CLASSIC TALES OF LIFE OUTDOORS

The Great Lakes Seasons Trilogy

More than eighty top outdoor and
nature writers share favorite tales of life
in the woods, fields, and waters of the
Upper Great Lakes Region. Select the
Seasons collection from your home
state, or check out all three. Each book
reflects the distinct landscape and literary character of its state. Each will
evoke memories of your own favorite
haunts and enhance your enjoyment of
the outdoors. All deserve a special place
beside the fireplace, or on the shelf at
your vacation getaway.

The Cabin Bookshelf

1234 Hickory Drive ■ Waukesha, WI 53186

MICHIGAN SEASONS
256 pages, hardcover
$22.95
ISBN 0-9653381-3-4

MINNESOTA SEASONS
248 pages, hardcover
$22.95
ISBN 0-9653381-4-2

WISCONSIN SEASONS
256 pages, hardcover
$22.95
ISBN 0-9653381-5-0

AVAILABLE AT YOUR LOCAL BOOKSTORE

CLASSIC TALES OF LIFE OUTDOORS

Minnesota Seasons

Edited by Scott Bestul

FEATURING STORIES AND ESSAYS BY:

John S. Allen	*Orval Lund*
Dennis Anderson	*Richard E. Massey*
Richard Behm	*Ted Nelson Lundrigan*
Greg Breining	*Judith Niemi*
Bob Cary	*Chris Niskanen*
Sam Cook	*Sigurd Olson*
Kent Cowgill	*Stuart Osthoff*
Rod Dimich	*Shawn Perich*
Larry M. Gavin	*Ron Schara*
Steve Grooms	*Doug Stange*
Paul Gruchow	*Mike Strandlund*
Jim Klobuchar	*Robert Treuer*
Gretchen Legler	*Joel M. Vance*
Peter M. Leschak	*John Weiss*

CLASSIC TALES OF LIFE OUTDOORS

Minnesota Seasons

Edited by
Scott Bestul

Illustrated by
Terry Maciej

Jacket photography by
Bill Marchel

The Cabin
Bookshelf

1234 Hickory Drive ■ Waukesha, WI 53186

MINNESOTA SEASONS
Classic Tales of Life Outdoors
Edited by Scott Bestul

Publisher's Cataloging in Publication
        (Prepared by Quality Books, Inc.)

Minnesota seasons/edited by Scott Bestul; illustrated by Terry
        Maciej; jacket photography by Bill Marchel. — 1st ed.
        p. cm.
        Preassigned LCCN: 98-70658
        ISBN: 0-9653381-4-2

        1. Hunting–Minnesota–Anecdotes.   2. Fishing–Minnesota–
Anecdotes.   3. Outdoor life–Minnesota–Anecdotes.   I.
Bestul, Scott.   II. Maciej, Terry.

        SK33.M56 1998   799'.09776
                                    QBI98-358

799
min   10-21-98

DEDICATION

To my father, who taught me
to love hunting and fishing
and the wild places we've visited
pursuing those sports;
and my mother, who showed me
the wonders of reading and writing.
You've defined and enriched my life
with your lessons.

SCOTT BESTUL
January 1998

ACKNOWLEDGEMENTS

Editing a book like this alone is as probable as casting a fly rod while holding it in your teeth. It's possible, but you're better off relying on your arms for some help. My arms came from publisher Ted Rulseh, who trusted an untried rookie with a major project; the fine authors included in this book, for the same reason; Kent Cowgill, who offered valuable advice and encouragement; Sandra Beth, who helped track down authors' work at the Winona Public Library; and my wife Shari, who has continually supported my career and sporting habits, even when she's not sure which is which. I hope the cast we've made here lays out beautifully.

JSB
January 1998

TABLE OF CONTENTS

FOREWORD *by Scott Bestul*
page xix

CONTENTS, CONTINUED

FOREWORD

Traveling not only allows you to see new places, but to see how people from those places view you. At a recent writers' conference in Florida, I introduced myself to a colleague and added, "I'm from Minnesota."

He laughed and nodded, "I could tell from the accent, yah-sure-you-betcha."

I could see the stereotype of my life dancing behind his smiling eyes: a frozen landscape for my backyard, walleye boat tucked in the garage, blond-haired wife and kids romping through the house in Scandinavian sweaters, Garrison Keillor volumes stacked on the bookshelf, a copy of the movie "Fargo" next to the VCR.

All right, so some of that stuff is true (none of your business which), but pigeon-holing Minnesotans is about as fruitless as looking for the state's signature region. Sure, most folks think Northwoods when the Gopher State comes to mind, but those who've spent time here know there's so much more. Pages from my hunting journal the last few seasons testify to Minnesota's diversity.

There are goose hunts near Lac qui Parle, where verdant farmland meets lush river bottoms to form waterfowl heaven. There was a moose hunt in the Boundary Waters Canoe Area, where my father and I paddled and portaged through a wilderness unmatched outside Canada or Alaska.

There were pheasant chases in the prairies near Marshall, grouse jaunts in the swamps near Bruno, deer stands in the woods outside Rochester, turkey roosts in the rolling hills of Lanesboro, bear baits north of Grand Marais, duck blinds on the Mississippi near Red Wing.

I experienced all this without ever buying a non-resident license, and I haven't even mentioned the fishing, camping, or canoeing.

The stories that appear in this book reflect Minnesota's diversity, as well as the talent of the state's writers. Twenty-eight of them are represented here. You'll find some who are nationally recognized, others known only within state boundaries, and a couple you've probably never heard of. There are newspaper writers, book authors, magazine scribes, even a couple of poets. They all responded to a request I made a while back: "Send me stories about why you hunt, fish, hike, and camp in Minnesota. Standard-issue, hook-and-bullet, how-to-where-to pieces are not appropriate."

Their response was both overwhelming and gratifying, and their stories describe the Minnesota outdoor experience much more eloquently than I can hope to. So, I'll let you enjoy Minnesota's seasons through their eyes. The ice is off the Mississippi, and I've got a walleye boat to get out of the garage, yah-sure-you-betcha!

Scott Bestul
Lewiston, Minnesota
January 1998

SPRING
We kept the windows rolled down and, as we raced through the night, the cab of the pickup swirled with the sweet smells of spring. I stuck my head out the window and closed my eyes, concentrating on the flow of smells from the passing countryside. The earth was thawing and alive, and nothing smelled better.

CHRIS NISKANEN
From *The Scent of Spring*

Hooked

ORVAL LUND
For Kent Cowgill

A trout sometimes leaps up
right out of the water
to take your fly, then dives
for rock, log, weeds, ledge,
anything shading sun
in its clear waterworld,
slicing your line in wild

geometry, hurling
its body into air
against your arcing rod.
Sometimes — face it — you end
life by taking it in hand
and cracking its head
so you can taste its gold,

but most of the time
you hold its silver
and release your death
from its jaw, full of awe
as it lies stunned on silt
slipping back into
its skin, vanishes.

It's then you wonder why
you're a creature who eats life
but also plays it in hand.
O Lord, help me to feel
the hook that plays me.
But so many times,
so many times, lets me go.

Reprinted from *Ordinary Days*, a chapbook from Dacotah Territory Press,
1996, and forthcoming in *Casting Lines*, New Rivers Press, 1999.

CHRIS NISKANEN

Chris Niskanen spent much of his childhood hunting and camping in the woods of northern Minnesota. After graduating from the University of Minnesota, he decided he wanted to get paid to pursue the things he loved most: hunting and fishing. He worked as an outdoors writer for daily newspapers in Iowa and Nevada before returning to Minnesota in 1993 as outdoors editor of the St. Paul Pioneer Press, *a position he still holds. He lives on a small lake near the St. Croix River with his hunting dog, Heidi.*

The Scent of Spring

CHRIS NISKANEN

> **On these springtime afternoons, the sun loosens winter's grip on the ground and, in turn, the smells of the warming earth jostle my memory. Juicy Fruit gum and bacon cooking on a campfire have the same effect, but not with the same clarity as springtime soil and clumpy leaves.**

I had the chance to smell dirt the other day. It was the good, loamy variety, thawed by a warm spring afternoon, rich in the odors of decay and the promise of life. I was in the hardwood forests of southeastern Minnesota, a few miles from Chatfield, lying next to a burr oak log. Stretched luxuriously on a soft mat of leaves and grasses, I was looking for any wild turkeys that might make themselves available during the upcoming hunting season.

Among hunters, this is called scouting, although there may be a fine line between loafing against a log on a spring day and scouting for turkeys. The important thing here is that the sun was streaming through the oaks and maples, warming my face and sending a recently arrived cardinal — a flash of crimson in the drab trees — into a frenetic serenade.

On these springtime afternoons, the sun loosens winter's grip on the ground and, in turn, the smells of the warming earth — the fecund soil, the moist and clumpy leaves — jostle my memory. Juicy Fruit gum and bacon cooking on a campfire have the same effect, but not with the same clarity as springtime soil and clumpy leaves.

I am whirled back to age twelve, living with my father in a stuccoed house on the edge of the small town of Deer River in northern Minnesota. The woods behind our house were filled with springtime mysteries: the tireless drumming grouse, always perched on the same log; the flowering apple trees, claw marks still fresh from last fall's foraging bear; and the wild asparagus, tucked away along an old fence row, far from the prying eyes of our neighbors.

As the sole asparagus picker in our family, I learned that asparagus was ripe when ticks appeared on my socks. Ticks and asparagus arrived in unison, or at least it seemed that way. A trip to the secret asparagus patch always meant a few minutes spent on the back porch, picking ticks off my pants legs.

Another rite of spring: In late April, my father and I would bomb around on the back roads, looking for spawning fish in the creeks. We weren't the only ones keeping vigil, either. You would pull up to a culvert and two or three cars might be parked along the road, the locals peering into the fast, cold water. There was nothing like a deep pool of spawning walleyes to draw a crowd. We ogled the bigger fish, their bulging bellies pressed against the gravel, tails swaying in rhythm with the current.

I remember the time-honored and persistent story of so-and-so (the name lost over the years), caught in the heinous act of spearing walleyes, then jumping into the creek to escape the game warden, who always got his man.

Speaking of spearing, one spring my father announced we were going sucker-spearing, a legal sport, the sucker being a rough fish and considered expendable. Suckers, my father explained, might be a trash fish to some people, but smoked over an alder fire they were delicious, better than salmon. Spearing and smoking suckers, he said, was something he did as a kid.

So we bought two spears, fashioned long wooden handles for them, and spent the better part of the weekend building a smokehouse out of a gutted refrigerator. We built it on concrete blocks, with a small stove at the bottom and a chimney on top. It might have looked like an old, white refrigerator on the outside, but to us it was the greatest smokehouse ever constructed.

The day before spearing season opened, we found a remote creek with hundreds of suckers crammed at the mouth of a culvert. Suckers were so thick we couldn't see the bottom of the pool. We figured the creek would be lined with other spearers the following day, but when we got there the next morning, we had the place to ourselves. My father stood on top of the culvert while I waded into the shallows downstream. The water, only days from having been snow, sent a shiver right to my scalp. When my father took a few stabs at the flotilla of fish, part of the school broke away, turned downstream, and steamed toward me. I felt the rubbery heads and snouts of dozens of suckers ramming my legs as I plunged the spear at their backs. It was easy to miss the swarming fish, as it is easy to shoot at, and miss, a duck flying in a flock. But, before long, we had filled several gunny sacks with suckers. We spent the rest of the afternoon cleaning them on the tailgate of the pickup.

Stacking the fillets in stone crocks, my grandmother soaked the fish in brine. The next day we loaded them on racks in the old refrigerator and stoked the stove with fresh-cut alder sticks. For weeks, we handed out smoked suckers to our friends, relatives and neighbors, and I remember toting them to school for lunch, their aromatic oils staining my brown paper bag.

Like most Minnesotans suddenly unleashed after a long winter, my father and I often spent spring looking for adventures. Perhaps that is how we ended up at the township dump one night, armed with a spotlight, two shotguns and a .22 magnum rifle. This time, our targets were rats. Like all kids, I was fascinated by the dump and the endless possibilities of reclaiming lost treasure. And although I had seen only an occasional rat at the dump, my imagination had locked on to their immense and insidious society amid the refuse. All this, coupled with my recent fascination with hunting, made a nighttime trip to the dump seem exciting.

Perhaps this is why my father told me to calm down when we arrived at the dump on a starlit night. He turned off the headlights of the pickup to avoid warning the rats of our arrival. We sat in the truck with the windows rolled down, listening. It was quiet, except for the sound of a tin can rattling. My father hooked up the spotlight, and I quietly slipped out of the pickup, the loaded .22 rifle in my hand.

When my father turned the spotlight on the mounds of debris, hundreds of beady eyes stared back. I aimed and fired. As quickly as I could remove the empty shell, the dump began to move. The rats' bodies were all shades of brown, black and white, and they hurled themselves, en masse, to the darkest corners of the pile. I emptied the gun, then watched the rats swarm over the garbage. Then I had the creepy sensation that they might turn on me.

I jumped into the pickup, shaking. My father was laughing; he said it didn't look like I had grazed a hair on a single rat. We tore out of the dump and never looked back. We kept the windows rolled down and, as we raced though the night, the cab of the pickup swirled with the sweet smells of spring. My father lit a cigarette; I stuck my head out the window and closed my eyes, concentrating on the flow of smells from the passing countryside.

There, a cattail swamp. Farther down the road, pines. A Christmas tree farm. Farther still, dirt. Yes, a farmer's freshly plowed field.

The earth was thawing and alive, and nothing smelled better.

Doug Stange is editor-in-chief of In-Fisher-man publications, including In-Fisherman *magazine, based in Brainerd, Minn. He has been a member of the* In-Fisherman *staff since 1981. In his tenure, he has written about almost every aspect of freshwater fishing, from ethical considerations to the principles of catching fish. He remains enthusiastic about traditionally popular species such as large-mouth bass and walleyes, but has also long been an advocate of the pleasures of fishing for less-utilized fish such as gar and carp. Doug lives in Brainerd with his wife and two children. Hunting and fishing are his main hobbies, but he also hits a fastball with the best of them in an old-timers baseball league that travels throughout Minnesota.*

DOUG STANGE

Reprinted by permission of The *In-Fisherman* magazine, Brainerd, Minn.

In Pursuit of Walleyes

DOUG STANGE

" Those midnight trips to catch those boot walleyes are so much less frequent today. Still, I feel each full moon rising in these bones. I still lie sleepless on many nights, wondering how busyness can interrupt such essence in anyone's life. "

Each time walleye graces the menu at our house, I'm reminded why I fish for them with a passion that reaches beyond common sense. They remain the essence of what a freshwater fish can be at the table, served so easily in a dozen different ways. And are they not even better — most memorable — as the focus of a traditional shore lunch? I thank God for each one of those rendezvous in the wilderness. And I include here an essential prayer for all of us before each season begins: the plea for yet another year rich with the company of friends, sitting near such a cooking fire, a morning of sweet pursuit just passed, an afternoon of fulfillment to come.

Yes, yes, other reasons call forth for the pursuit of this fine fish. Aspects of the process of pursuit can become an integral part of one's life, even life-changing, or at least, in some sense, life-defining. I am who I am in small part because for so many years, during my most formative years of fishing, I spent thirty nights each season shuffling around in waders at the mouths of current areas, casting for those walleye monsters that move silently through the shallows in search of bait fish.

I stood there hoping and scheming, so much alone with my thoughts, until I began to find a way to make the catching happen. Drinking countless cups of coffee by the light of a quarter moon. Some nights, rain, sleet or snow pelting my back. Standing, too, on those perfect nights, the smell of smoldering leaves in the air, a harvest moon rising in the east. And, in other ways, defining and redefining the process — the rod, the reel, the line, the lures, the spots, the time of year — until that process was a fine science of sorts.

Soon enough, too, having spent the time, paid enough dirty dues, it began to work so well — those senses so finely tuned in the darkness, so abruptly interrupted by a "walleye pause" in a dead-slow retrieve. And then kneeling there with one of those monsters at net, flashlight beam reflecting the life in those marble eyes. In early years, a fish for the wall. Soon enough, those fish released, the satisfaction in a photo. These days, no more than a smile and a salute to send the big ones on their way. Smaller fish, though, still fare well at my table. Even two smaller fish, the focus of a fine meal.

Those midnight trips to catch those boot walleyes are so much less frequent today. Still, I feel each full moon rising in these bones. I still lie sleepless on many nights, wondering how busyness can interrupt such essence in anyone's life. My grandpa taught me, though, that we fish, too, if only for a moment and at some distance, when we have hard-won experiences to remember and the hope of more to come.

The same intense fishing and learning processes were for me repeated for a half-dozen or more essential approaches that define basic walleye fishing. Hundreds of hours spent at night during spring, and then fall, longline trolling plugs over shallow shoals. Weekend trips to small dams in late winter to find walleyes in marginal walleye rivers, bouncing jig-and-minnow combos in eddies in the tailwater. Trips, too, to do much the same in major tailwater areas on the Mississippi and Missouri rivers, bobbing along in one of those first classic boats, a 315 Lund. (I'm reminded that those early days began the long, slow search by a world of walleye anglers for the perfect walleye boat.)

Soon enough began the season-long sessions of discovering the secrets of live-bait rigging with crawlers, leeches, chubs and water dogs — those trips interspersed with journeys to explore the newly formed reservoirs in the Dakotas: first, drifting plugs in the boiling tailwaters in May, and then in June, drifting or trolling over those huge reservoir flats with early day spinner rigs and crawlers.

Later in the season, when the fishing turned difficult on natural lakes, I twitched surface baits at twilight to scratch a walleye or two holding tight in heavy weed cover. Even today, this remains a technique not fully explored and certainly seldom written about. We also used Buck Perry methods, trolling Spoonplugs, Mudbugs or Hellbenders at speeds that puzzle the minds of anglers today. Such techniques seem to have been lost in time.

Of course, it was shorecasting and longlining again in fall. Then, to finish open-water season, at least a week of pushing a duck boat across an iced-up bay to reach open water to cast and swim Cap's Rock-A-Roo jigs over a rock bar, which, by the way, was just where those old walleyes were when first ice finally finished the open-water season. Then, what else was there to do each weekend of winter than have a morning and evening affair with walleyes on ice? And finally, late winter in the air, the cycle began again.

You see, a good portion of my life has revolved around walleyes. Looking back, I would not have had it any other way. And it is hopeless to expect change now. Last night was another of those nights. When I arrived home at midnight, a couple of strips of bacon hit the pan. Bacon finished, a little butter added to season the bacon oil, then the fillets dusted in flour and corn meal, plus salt, cayenne and black pepper. Three minutes passing, turn those fillets, and add a couple of eggs to fry alongside. Won't be long now, so pour that glass of wine, tear off a hunk of bread. Relive the night passing, and toast days of pursuit to come.

RON SCHARA

Ron Schara has been an outdoor journalist for three decades. He recently retired from the outdoors staff of the Minneapolis Star Tribune, *but he remains a free-lance columnist for the paper. He now devotes more of his time to television and radio. His TV program, "Minnesota Bound," airs on KARE-TV, Channel 11, in the Twin Cities. His national program, "Call of the Wild," is seen on The Outdoor Channel cable outlet. Ron is also seen nationally on ESPN on "Backroads with Ron & Raven," and his "Call of the Wild" radio network can be heard five times per week on more than thirty Midwest stations. Ron grew up in northeast Iowa's rugged bluff country. He holds degrees in both journalism and fish and wildlife biology.*

Understanding Wild Turkeys

RON SCHARA

" The turkey hunter walks along in the woods, chirping like a willing hen to entice a gobbler within range. If a gobbler believes the offer, he seeks out the calling sound, only to find a loaded shotgun. Somewhere in all that, there has to be a lesson in life. "

This Guide to Understanding Wild Turkeys is unauthorized and unpredictable, which is appropriate considering the subject. It is written by a fellow who, twenty-five years ago, was hunkered on a pine ridge posing as a turkey hunter. Such longevity makes him a qualified turkey expert, although he knows these is no such thing as a turkey expert.

What is the wild turkey? It is a North American gallinaceous bird, which means it is related to chickens. But only the chicken is brain dead. The wild turkey also is related to the domestic turkey, which also happens to be dumber than a fencepost, thanks to the domestication process. A wild hen turkey has a gray-blue feathered head and weighs about ten pounds. An adult tom turkey has a red-white-and-blue skinhead and might weigh eighteen to twenty-five pounds or more. Despite pea-sized brains, both sexes of wild turkey have maintained intelligence and are smarter than the average viewer of television sitcoms.

What is wild turkey hunting? It is an X-rated sport. Gobbler (male) calls to hen (female) turkey for spring seduction purposes. Hens usually ignore advances. The turkey hunter walks along in the woods, chirping like a willing hen to entice a gobbler within range. If a gobbler believes the offer, he seeks out the calling sound, only to find a loaded shotgun. Somewhere in all that, there has to be a lesson in life. Beyond the turkey tabloids, the truth is real turkeys seldom fall for the pseudo-chirpings of woodland hanky-panky. Nationally, hunting success rates rarely exceed twenty-five percent.

What does X-rated turkey talk sound like? It begins with a whispered chirp, a tree call, and rises to a cackle of delight. A lonesome hen says, "Yelp, yelp." Lots of harsh yelps mean "gather up." Sometimes the hen cutts, which sounds like a marble bouncing on a glass slate. Sometimes she purrs like a kitten. Usually she keeps her beak shut. The gobbler has only one thing on his mind in springtime. So it just gobbles.

What happens during a hunt? When you hear a turkey close by, you sit next to a large tree with your knees up to rest the shotgun. Then, you call and hold still. The gobbler might or might not answer. A few minutes later, you'll feel something crawling in the lower reaches of your back. This might be a wood tick, or it might be your imagination. Since you don't know, you reach to scratch. At that moment, the gobbler comes into view, sees your scratching hand, says "sputt" and departs unscathed.

Why do you want to shoot a poor, defenseless gobbler? There is no such bird.

Are they elusive? If I get a turkey permit next year, the first thing that gobbles is going to die.

You sound like a teed-off turkey hunter. Just joking. Hey, we're talking about the grandest of all game birds. Wild turkey hunting isn't a season. It's a lifestyle. Turkey admirers don't need to shoot a bird. It's the relationship they seek.

What's the attraction? For a few glorious moments during a sunrise, you're a third party in the lives of wild turkeys. That and the sights and sounds of a waking woods, a deer in the gray light, the hoot of a barred owl, the twirps of so many unknowns in a waking forest. It's all of that and, oh, just find out for yourself.

Why do turkey hunters dress like commandoes? Turkey hunters typically are late to mature. Another reason is that the wild turkey's eyesight and hearing are so exceptional; the senses are always underrated. The only thing a wild turkey can't see is the other side of the tree it's standing under. The bird's hearing is so sensitive it's said a gobbler knows your location when it hears your call. Calls that are too loud are sometimes held suspect by a gobbler. Most real turkey hens are more discreet.

Why do you write about wild turkeys every year? I can't help it.

Since 1992, Dennis Anderson has been an out-doors columnist for the Minneapolis Star Tribune. *For fifteen years before that, he wrote an outdoor column for the* St. Paul Pioneer Press. *Dennis was born in North Dakota and*

DENNIS ANDERSON

grew up in the Upper Peninsula of Michigan. He received a bachelor's degree in English from the University of Minnesota-Morris and a master's in journalism from the U of M in Minneapolis. Through his newspaper column, he founded the conservation group Pheasants Forever in 1982. In 1989, he was a Pulitzer Prize finalist for a year-long investigation of America's declining duck population. Dennis, his wife Janice and their sons Trevor and Cole live on a small farm on the Wisconsin side of the St. Croix River.

Reprinted by permission of the *Minneapolis Star Tribune.*

Buster

DENNIS ANDERSON

> **As best I could determine from Trevor's description, Buster was a sunfish. It could also have been a bass, given the vagaries of communicating with a three-year-old.**

Only fish of the XXL variety are given names. Moby Dick is one example. Jaws is another. So is Buster, a sunfish-whale cross that transfixes my son, Trevor, at bedtime. Trevor, age three, learned of Buster in a book. The fish's story is more spare, but not unlike that told about Santiago, Hemingway's protagonist in The Old Man and the Sea. Man seeks fish, achieves some success, is transformed by the quest.

The difference in Trevor's story is that upon catching Buster and bolting him to his bedroom wall, Trevor relaunches his imaginary boat, and he again is on the water in search of Buster — assuming I'm willing to read the book another time.

Through a thousand readings of the tale, Trevor had demanded no more than its retelling. Then, the other morning, something snapped and Trevor awoke with malice in his little heart. Over oatmeal, he announced he was prepared to hold up in Daddy's boat until Buster could be accounted for. Thrusting his Snoopy fishing rod toward his mother, he demanded to be taken, as he put it, "shishing."

This happened at 7:30 a.m., when I was two hundred miles down the road, horse trailer in tow. A friend, a bull rider, is in a self-imposed rodeo recovery program and is learning to avoid trips like these. I'm headed for a similar meltdown, but I'm not there yet.

So that today, after five hours in a truck, four hours on horses and another five-hour drive home, I was informed by Trevor and his mother — who by then was thrusting the Snoopy rod in my direction — that this fish Buster was in need of immediate attention.

"Catch him or die trying," I was told.

I put in a call to Irv Rubbelke. Irv is a friend from St. Paul who has children, grandchildren and great-grandchildren. He would understand. Plus, he's a great fisherman and inventor of the Tattle-Tail bobber.

"Be here in the morning," I said.

Which is how Trevor, Irv and I found ourselves on a small body of water in search of Buster, a fish that, as best I could determine from Trevor's description, was a sunfish. It could also have been a bass, given the vagaries of communicating with a three-year-old. But bass season was not yet open. So I strongly supported the notion that Buster was indeed a sunnie. Pointing to a picture of such a fish, I would say, "That's Buster. I'm sure it is."

It took Irv and me a while to find fish. When we did, Trevor already had consumed a peanut butter sandwich, an apple, and a bottle of juice. He had also twice demanded to be put ashore so he could throw rocks. Mostly, though, he insisted on driving the boat.

"You're not the captain, Dad. I am," he said.

On the plus side, he had not yet needed his diaper changed.

"With luck," I told Irv, "he'll be back in his mother's arms, Buster on a stringer, before that happens."

The first fish we caught, a small sunnie, was not Buster. The second, a bass, wasn't Buster, either. The third, a much nicer sunnie, could have been Buster, Trevor said, but probably was his brother. Or mom.

"Buster's out there somewhere," he said.

Trevor's Snoopy rod was rigged with a bobber and tube jig, and baited with a waxworm. And, like Irv and me, Trevor was catching fish fairly regularly, reeling them in, for the most part, on his own, before tossing them in the direction of the livewell. He was having fun. But two hours had passed, and no Buster.

Then Trevor's bobber disappeared. No nibble, no concentric circles issuing from red-and-white plastic. Only the bobber vanishing and Trevor's line coming tight.

"It's Buster!" Trevor shouted.

Trevor's bedtime story has changed since then. Now I tell him how he and Daddy and Irv went fishing, how Trevor ate a peanut butter sandwich and an apple, how he drank a bottle of juice, and how he insisted on being the boat's captain. Then I tell him that his bobber disappeared and that he reeled in the biggest sunfish of the day.

Then Trevor says, "And that was Buster."

PAUL GRUCHOW

Paul Gruchow lives in Northfield, Minn., teaches at Concordia College in Moorhead during the school year, and teaches summers for St. Olaf College at Wolf Ridge Environmental Learning Center on Lake Superior's North Shore. He also owns a farm in southwestern Minnesota, "so I feel at home in every corner of the state." His wife is an attorney, his son is finishing high school, and his daughter is a college student in Oregon. He has published six books, most recently Boundary Waters: The Grace of the Wild. *When not teaching or writing, Paul likes to cook, garden and walk. His current project is hiking the Continental Divide from Canada to Mexico.*

Five Incarnations of a Mink

PAUL GRUCHOW

> I followed my father's instructions and felt myself drawn nearer to the wildness I sought. I imagined that I was an Indian boy living long ago and that the instruction I was getting was ultimately in the art of survival. I wished to need to know how to survive by my wits in nature, as boys once did.

In young adolescence I took up the trapping of the furbearers that lived in the river bottom below our farm. I learned to catch muskrats, skunks and weasels. I subscribed to *Fur, Fish & Game* and dreamed of living someday in a cabin in the Adirondacks. In these dreams I was always alone, it was always winter, and I was always out on snowshoes tending my traplines. I imagined an evergreen world, silent and unsullied. I was not after the pelts, nor the money I got from selling them. I had to be nagged to skin the creatures I caught and to see to stretching the pelts and scraping and drying them. Once I had caught a creature, I lost interest in it.

What I really wanted was a share of the wildness in the creatures I pursued. I wanted the thrill of thinking like something wild; of guessing where I would be if I were, say, a weasel; of imagining things that might then arouse my curiosity; of thinking just where I would step. I wanted to be able to read the landscape in the way that a weasel does, to share its way of seeing, to assume its language. I was like a blind man imagining sight or a deaf man hearing. I yearned for the leap of imagination that would send me off into the unimaginable wilderness.

The day came when I thought I might match wits against a mink, the smartest, the most elusive of the wild creatures I knew. I had spent many years watching the life in my valley, but the mink was a creature of the night, and I had never chanced even to catch a glimpse of one. Nevertheless, I knew they existed, and I knew where. The signs of them, which I had learned to read, were all around.

My father showed me how to set a trap on a slide so that when I caught my mink, it would drown quickly. He showed me where to position a trap for a mink, how to follow the trail of one along a stream bank, what sort of obstruction would force it down into the water, where it would likely move when so diverted, how to construct an artificial diversion, how to conceal a trap without demobilizing it, how to use a bit of musk oil as a lure and where to apply it in relation to the trap. I followed my father's instructions and felt myself drawn nearer to the wildness I sought. I imagined that I was an Indian boy living long ago and that the instruction I was getting was ultimately in the art of survival. I wished to need to know how to survive by my wits in nature, as boys once did.

I set my traps and tended them. When they failed to produce, I made adjustments. Once or twice I found a sprung trap, which encouraged me. But the mink remained elusive. A new season came, and I set out my traps again. Every one was aimed at a mink. I could not be bothered anymore with such mundane prey as muskrats. I did catch two or three muskrats that season — quite by accident — but no mink.

One day near the end of the season there was warning of a blizzard. My father told me to pull in my traps while I still could, but I ignored the advice. Before I could make a last check of them, the snow started to fall so heavily and the winds to drive so fiercely that there could be no thought of going down into the valley. The snow fell all that day and the next, and the wind raged for two nights and three days before there was peace again.

I didn't get back to the traps I had set until the snow melted the next spring. I found one of them out of place. I yanked its stake up, and when I began to pull on its chain, I realized that there was more than a trap at the other end of it. The little stream was swollen with the debris of the spring flood, and it was a nasty business to get the catch untangled and up into the air. When the trap finally drew up, I saw the mink on the end of it, a fine buck mink in what had obviously been a splendid dark winter coat.

I was wild with excitement. But when I unsnared the mink, I saw that my slide had not worked properly. The mink had not drowned right away. It had nearly gnawed its caught leg through before death had come. I understood that the creature had been caught in the first storm of winter. Perhaps, intent on finding shelter, it had been a bit less wary than usual. It had made a desperate attempt to free itself, had nearly succeeded, and then had succumbed to the storm.

I carried the carcass home, skinned it, fleshed the pelt, stretched it, hung it up to dry. I tossed the bones to the barn cats, who stripped them of flesh before the night was out. Then I took myself away to a private place and faced the sadness that had swollen up inside me. I did not understand the sadness then or ever. The best I could make of it was that I felt a kind of shame for having taken advantage of the mink I had so admired. I could in a sense partake of its wildness; with enough patience I could make out its ways and deliver the creature into my own hands. But the consequence was, and always would be, I saw, some kind of destruction.

One spring day years later I went down to the dam at Blue Mounds State Park in southwestern Minnesota to watch the annual carp migration. In the springtime, like the fabled salmon of the Northwest, the carp in the park's lower pond try to make their way up a tiny stream, over a dam and into the upper pond. The dam rises six or eight feet above the spring water level of the upper pond. It presents a formidable barrier to a leaping carp.

The length of the odds does not discourage the carp. Time and again I have watched one use the strength of its tail to throw itself up into the air. It lands upon the jagged rocks somewhere forward of the position where it started, coming down with a slap. Then it is either swept back into the pool it started from or heaves itself up into the air again, trying another advance upon the waterfall. The efforts of an hour might bring it at last to the base of the concrete dam, where it flings itself again and again toward the top of the dam until, in tiredness or miscalculation, it makes a jump that causes it to fall out of range of the highest holding pool. Then the carp slides and bangs down into the stream again, from which it mounts a new assault on the dam.

As I stood that spring day at the edge of the uppermost pond, caught up in the ordeal of the carp, I became aware that I was not alone, although I could see no other creature nearby. A minute or two passed. A small carp almost at my feet made a feeble assault on the mountainous dam, failed, and fell with a splash back into the pool. Momentarily stunned from the fall, it hesitated. In that instant, a dark creature lunged forward, snared the fish in its claws, latched onto it with its jaws, and disappeared into the thicket of rushes at the edge of the pool. The whole action took a few seconds. It was like the brief shadow of a cloud passing.

I saw the mink emerge with the fish in its mouth and disappear again into the young green vegetation. I pursued it for a long time. My effort was as futile as that of the carp. Water fell over the dam, crashed down upon the rocks with a roar, and ran off in the mysterious direction of the mink.

It was high winter on Rush Lake in northwestern Iowa. The landscape was as clean and spare as any the prairie winter offers: signs of a mouse, here and there the tracks of a pheasant, at a few of the muskrat houses on the lake open breathing holes indicating residents within, a pair of cottontail rabbits in the shelter of the shore, a shrike shouting from a treetop, chickadees, in the distance the calling of a crow. The wind had piled the snow in waves and scalloped them. They looked like the beached and empty shells of sea creatures.

I stopped at one of the largest muskrat houses in the middle of the lake to look for signs of occupancy. In the fresh snow around the rather large air hole, I saw the footprints of a mink. The mink had not entered the house. It had merely paused there to investigate; then it had urinated at the edge of the hole, dropped its scat, and gone on its way. In a few feet, the trail of the mink disappeared into the anonymity of bare ice. The droppings on the house were full of muskrat hair.

I wandered until dusk, drinking in the clean sharpness of the winter air. When the sun set, the sky was almost colorless, as understated as everything else in winter except the wind. I came out upon the road again and climbed a knoll toward the highway. The light was falling rapidly. As I neared my car I saw, in the shadows ahead, a mink. It turned, stared at me for a long, deliberate second, disappeared. It was for all the world like a wink.

I tarried for a night along Lake Superior's North Shore, where craggy cliffs meet an oceanic expanse of chill, deep, ice-blue water, a coastline worthy of the Pacific or the Atlantic. After dinner I sauntered along the pebbled beach and out onto a spit of rock, seeking nothing in particular but to idle away an hour.

I admired the fist-sized blue and gray and sometimes black beach stones, rounded and smooth from centuries of churning in the now gentle, now thunderous, ever relentless waves. They seemed fallen and solidified pieces of sky, so much the same color were they as the blues and grays in the distance, where earth and heaven met vaguely, shimmeringly over the lake. I looked into pools of water caught in shallow basins in the polished granite above the beach, ached like a surfacing whale, hoping in vain to encounter some creature staring back at me. I admired the tiny pin cushion plants blooming in the crevices of rock and the asters making a lavender splash on the leeward side of the spit, where, diverted by it, a river ran its last thousand yards parallel to the shore before finding an opportunity and slipping silently into Superior. A man and his dog fished just above the bar of the outlet for steelhead trout. The trout seemed not to be biting. The fisherman alternately tended his line and his dog, for whom he now and then tossed a whitened stick of driftwood, which the dog, bounding into the current of the river, fetched back. The man, perhaps, fished as Thoreau's neighbors did, "much more in the Walden Pond of their own natures, and baited their hooks with darkness." Overhead, gulls wheeled, crying in the salty voices of the sea, which these waters would at last reach in some future century.

The sun setting over the thousand-foot ridge behind me infused the sky with a salmon-colored light. It echoed in the granite's rosy crystals of quartz. I zipped my jacket against the evening breeze and turned back toward the car. Along the way, I became aware of a slight motion at the periphery of my vision. Pausing to take account of it, I found myself staring into the eyes of two baby mink, their dark coats fuzzy with the fine hair of infancy, their big eyes wide, their heads cocked and ears raised in curiosity, but with bodies tensed and legs crouched to flee. In a moment, they lost nerve and scampered and tumbled away.

I followed at a discreet distance. Naively, they led me to their den in a tumble of boulders at a place where ice had worked a crack in the spit and pried it apart. A pair of shrubby willows had taken root there and screened the place from the public parking lot just across the narrow river. The kits vanished into an opening among the boulders, but they could not stay hidden for long. Soon they peered out of crevices, all eyes, and, when they saw that I saw them, ducked to safety again. We played peek-a-boo.

For a few minutes I enjoyed the game as much as they, and then I grew uneasy with the fear that my presence might compromise them. I turned and circled to the top of the spit to take my leave. But I desired one more glimpse of them. When I looked down, I saw not the babies, but the mother. Her fur was sleek and dripping, and she was half-carrying, half-dragging a lake trout toward the den. The fish was half again as long as she and thicker in the body. I could not imagine how she might have caught it. Mink are fierce and swift, but trout are equally keen-eyed and wary. Perhaps the trout was carrion found along the shore or had been released by the fisherman downriver and seized while it was still disoriented or disabled. At any rate, it was quite dead, and the mink was so occupied in hauling it home that she did not notice me. I watched until the mink retreated into the shadow of the willows.

By then, dusk had fallen. The air had the graininess of some black-and-white photographs, and the lake looked more like a pool of light than like a body of water, a dreamy and transfigured landscape in which floated apparitions of mink and fish, of rock and flower, of birth and death, of day and night, of water and sky. Across the lake the evening star appeared, a stab of light in the taut stillness.

———————————————

I descended the Minong Ridge on Isle Royale at the place where it crosses one branch of the upper reaches of Washington Creek and was just about to set my right boot onto a steppingstone when a dark, lithe, long-tailed animal slipped around an alder and disappeared into a thicket of shrubs. I had a second's look at it, if that, before it vanished. A cursory exploration in the direction it had gone revealed no readable footprint.

Perhaps if I had not been so intent on getting to Windigo before the store closed (I did not yet know that it hadn't opened), if there had not been a boat to meet in the morning, if I had not committed myself to obligations that bound me to meeting it, perhaps if I had ever learned to travel freely, or believed more deeply in the opportunities the moment brings, I might have unburdened myself of my pack and gone in search of that fleeting image. But I didn't. I looked where the creature had gone, replayed the image of it in my eye, stepped to the opposite shore of the little stream and trudged uphill, beads of sweat gathering in the small of my back, hoping that some less fleeting presence might appear along the way to compensate for the loss.

I thought it might have been an ermine in a dark summer coat, or a mink, or even an otter, although it seemed small for that. Most likely, I decided, the creature was a mink. Later that day, I would claim to have seen a mink and to have been pleased at the sight of it, but it was the kind of lie we tell when we are disappointed. The truth was, I had seen a fleeting shadow for a brief moment, a thin thread of experience, and had embroidered it into a story. We tell stories like this all the time; our lives consist of the sum of them.

I can see the moment even now, a long time later, just as if it had freshly happened: the glance to the left, where the tan water ran through the green stems of a marsh marigold bright with golden flower, the flurry of motion, the flash of visual data, long, lithe, brown or black, with tail. It remains one of my most vivid impressions of Isle Royale. I have stored it with a hundred thousand other impressions just like it of a thousand other places. I want to extract them, make them solid, and render them as something concrete: a collage maybe, or a quilt. See, I could then say, this is the essence of wildness. This is what we must not forget: how brief life is, how unexpected, how little of it we glimpse, how rapidly it changes.

I, like the next person, struggle to make sense of what I have heard and seen. I tell stories about wild places, as if I had discovered anything at all. If I told the truth, everything I described would be indistinct and on the run. This would be a true picture of the wild places I have known, including those of my own heart: I would be standing at the center of the frame, and at its edges would be seen the tails of things, mysterious and alluring, their owners dashing for cover.

Bob Cary, age 76, started outdoor writing sixty years ago with the Herald-News *in Joliet, Ill., after serving in combat with the U.S. Marines,*

BOB CARY

World War II, South Pacific. He married in 1948 to late wife Lillian, who paddled bow in the canoe while the couple fished, hunted and camped over much of North America. Daughter Barbara Hall lives in Duluth and daughter Marge Kaveney in Houston, Tex. After nine years as outdoor editor of the Chicago Daily News, *Bob moved to Ely in 1966 to found a wilderness canoe guiding and outfitting business, which he ran for eight years. He is now editor of the* Ely Echo *newspaper and a freelance writer and illustrator for outdoor and conservation publications. He is also the author of five books. He spends his summers on the canoe trails and is a competitive cross-country ski racer in winter. He considers himself "the luckiest man alive."*

Who Shot Reuben Wood?

BOB CARY

" What made the Reuben Wood so effective was the subject of endless debate. Conjecture held that it resembled a bass hatchling, fair game for larger cannibals. Perhaps it was simply close enough to the schooling shiners and chubs that glittered in the shoals. "

Once upon a time, long, long ago, nobody ever heard of a Grey Wulff, Dahlberg Diver, Dun Variant, Wooly Worm, Brown Bivisible, Horner's Silver Shrimp, Green Ghost, Atherton's Dark Nymph or many of the myriad other patterns deemed necessary for today's fly angling success.

Back in the late 1920s and early '30s, fly casters relied on perhaps six to a dozen "standards," which may or may not have resembled some type of aquatic life. These included the Brown Hackle, Grey Hackle, Black Gnat, White Miller, Wickham's Fancy, Red Ibis, Grizzly King, Montreal, Lord Baltimore, Parmacheene Belle and Yellow Sally, to name a few. Oh, yes, and Reuben Wood.

Reuben Wood? Scarcely a fly caster of this era will recognize the name. But some six or seven decades back, in a somewhat more contemplative and traditional era, Reuben Wood was considered a rather effective captor of speckled trout and a deadly deceiver of river bass. Which takes us to the matter at hand, to those Midwest farm streams where many of my generation passed through adolescence to manhood, when not encumbered by such distractions as school and earning a living. ("Manhood" may not be politically correct, but it is certainly historically valid. I do not recall meeting a single female fly caster in that whole era. Possibly there was some restrictive law concerning streamside gender that was repealed during the civil rights movement, but I am not sure.)

In any event, as boys and men, we diligently pursued those red-eyed, jut-jawed smallmouth warriors with a singleness of purpose, usually starting our forays with a Reuben Wood tied to a silkworm gut leader. What made this pattern so effective was the subject of endless debate.

The fly was tied on a size 6, 8 or 10 hook in the somewhat revolutionary streamer style: white chenille body, red butt (some preferred wisps of gray mallard tail), brown hackle and gray fox wing. Conjecture held that the gray fox, with its dark forepart and white tip, resembled a bass hatchling, fair game for larger cannibals. Perhaps it was simply close enough to the schooling shiners and chubs that glittered in the shoals. Or, as some said, maybe it resembled a frantic soft-shelled crawfish scooting backward in panic to avoid capture.

In any event, the pattern was favored by many. However, if bass were active and Rube failed to produce, we shifted to other patterns, albeit reluctantly. Rube was not the only fly that caught fish.

An instance burned into my memory concerned a blistering July afternoon on the Fox River when the shoreline willows and elms hung dispiritedly, and the pungent odor of sun-baked mud permeated the atmosphere. Reasoning that any intelligent bass would seek the coolest depths, I was whipping a quiet pool just upstream from a substantial riffle.

My father was standing in the riffle, drifting nightcrawlers ineffectively into the eddies with his seven-foot tubular steel "fly rod," a cumbersome affair that he never, to my knowledge, ever used to cast a fly. Other than a number of biting sand flies and some tired-looking dragonflies, little was stirring. A nearby great blue heron, standing on one leg in the tepid shallows, appeared to be in a state of slumber.

At length, my father waded up to me, lit his usual cigarette, and inquired, "Any luck?"

Nope." This in a somewhat annoyed manner, since I was well aware that he could see I had no stringer in the water.

"What're you using?"

"Reuben Wood."

"Um ... try anything else?"

"What for?"

"Let's see your fly box."

I hated this. I felt my father had no more business delving into my tackle than I had into his. But I pulled out the box and popped it open. He fingered a few feathered specimens, then singled out a size 10 Red Ibis.

"Try this," he proclaimed with authority.

First, I was well aware that my knowledge and skill with flies were superior to his, and that no bass in his right mind would rise to such a gaudy offering of minuscule size on such a hot, clear day. Reluctantly, I clipped off the Rube Wood and tied on the Ibis, resolving to show the old man the error of his thinking.

Briefly working out a length of line, I laid the Ibis up and across the pool with no particular target in mind, allowed it to drift momentarily, picked up the slack, and started it back in a series of erratic tugs.

From somewhere in the shadowy depths arose a dark form that flashed over in a burst of copper brilliance, smashed the fly, and dove.

"See?" my father gloated.

Ten minutes later, the bass came gasping to hand, all fifteen gorgeous inches of him. With a twitch, I disengaged the fly and released the fish, more an exercise in revenge than altruism. My father was of the old school: whatever you caught you kept. And ate. I knew that letting such a trophy go would scald his psyche. He said nothing, but I knew, with some satisfaction, that he could never forgive such an affront.

The turn of the century and a few decades beyond was sometimes described by elderly anglers as the golden age of fly fishing. There was no such thing as spin casting. For sure, the Meek brothers and other watchmakers in Kentucky had developed rather intricate casting reels, devices copied and widely marketed, which could be matched to stubby split bamboo rods to hurl half-ounce wooden lures with fair distance and accuracy. Unfortunately, in those frequent instances when thumb and spool failed to coordinate, the line overran, and an incredible tangle occurred.

Fly tackle was readily available at a modest price; it was easier to master and far more effective.

River smallmouth bass fishing was essentially fly fishing in the honorable and historic tradition. Even live bait devotees preferred fly rods to deliver their offerings.

Perhaps because the clear, relatively pollution-free streams of that era contained a bounteous supply of fish, or because angling pressure was minimal, our success was, in hindsight, rather phenomenal. Certainly one could wade a half-mile of stream without meeting another angler, at least on weekdays, and score plenty of fish. In any event, those old standards took a terrible toll.

Since there were relatively few patterns, we knew them by heart and could discuss their merits with certainty. Who tied the best patterns was then, as now, a matter of considerable speculation.

My old Scoutmaster, Paul Ohman, tied the finest Reuben Woods and, when opportunity afforded, I tried to cajole him out of a specimen or two. He was also an incredible source of information on flies and fly fishing. In later years I have come to suspect that Paul gleaned much of his knowledge from the historic book, *Favorite Flies and Their Histories*, by Mary Orvis Marbury, daughter of the legendary Charles Frederick Orvis of rod-making and fly-tying fame.

The book delves into favored patterns of tiers back into the 1800s, most of whom relied on few "standards." Included in this intriguing book are accounts of how flies were named, such as the Lord Baltimore, black and orange, with a touch of jungle cock. Apparently, two angler-tiers from Baltimore, Maryland, originally devised this fly as black and yellow, but later found that when modified with orange, it contained the heraldic colors of the British Lord. It was, and is, a stunning combination, but no one I ever knew caught much on it.

Some of those early patterns had no relationship to anything swimming in or flying over lake or stream. They were tied simply to suit the eye of the tier. If they happened to catch fish, so much the better. Certainly, many flies were tied, however, to resemble aquatic insects. Early American fly casters, like their European cousins, were knowledgeable concerning drakes, stoneflies, caddis, and other forms, along with terrestrial dwellers. It was just that the Europeans seemed to get more technical, while the Americans tended to engage in more whimsy.

Before the early 1900s, that whimsy resulted in all manner of outlandish creations categorized as "bass flies." Since there were no bass in Europe, there was no background, no tradition. The sky was the limit. Even the Orvis family, perhaps the nation's most skilled craftsmen in fly tackle, produced a host of monstrosities — huge, multicolored, winged wet flies tied on 2/0 hooks or larger. No doubt, they accounted for a few low-I.Q. largemouth bass, but they had little appeal to river smallmouth. I knew several old timers in the 1920s who had samples of these enormous bass flies in their tackle boxes, where they invariably languished.

Unfortunately, much of that whimsy has vanished with today's emphasis on exactness and effectiveness. Flies like the Reuben Wood nearly got washed away in the process.

It is still a superb streamer fly for smallmouth bass. I hark back to many days on many streams with Rube. My favorite rod was an eight-foot, four-ounce split bamboo Winchester, an exceedingly slow and willowy stick. By today's graphite standards, it would be derisively described as a "noodle rod."

But my, how I loved that Winchester. It was given to me by an old trout master from Michigan's Upper Peninsula, but it was eminently tailored for river bass. One had to concentrate on the pickup and backcast, stripping line to overcome the slowness, and then lean into the forward thrust. It was almost like casting in slow motion, but that rod would lay out a fly with superb accuracy and deposit it with scarcely a ripple. I missed many strikes due to slowness in response, but even foot-long smallmouth were terrors on that wand. How I grieved the day I broke it, an occurrence of my fault alone, one that brings a stab of pain even now, almost sixty years later.

But that was another era, and Reuben Wood has been somewhat moribund, lo these many years. Well, almost. There are still a dozen or so in my fly box, creations I replenish annually and use for better or worse. In August 1991, my wife, Lil, and I were on Alaska's Tsiu River, down the coast from Cordova, through the courtesy of bush pilot-outfitter Pat Magie. The river, Magie said, from its ocean mouth back a mile or two, was loaded with silver salmon from eight to fourteen pounds. His twin-engine Beechcraft delivered us to a rough but comfortable streamside tent camp where we shared accommodations and dining facilities with a half-dozen California anglers, two guides and a cook .

My wife, a spin tackle enthusiast, immediately strode to the nearest riffle where one could observe up to eight or ten salmon resolutely wedging their way upstream to complete their life cycle. Tiring of watching her hook and battle several salmon on hardware (which also required me to tail the fish and release them), I hurried back to camp and made the acquaintance of a fly caster who, it was said, had considerable experience with silvers.

Let it be known, at this point, that my experience with salmon on a fly rod was limited entirely to what was available in various books, magazines, and videos. I had no real salmon tackle. I was armed with a nine-foot bass rod, matching weight-forward line, and a supply of leaders, but no earthly idea what to tie on the terminal end. From what I had seen in color prints, salmon flies were extraordinarily large and gaudy.

When I explained that my knowledge was limited mainly to Midwest bass, the gentleman from California smiled kindly, opened one of several oversize tackle boxes, and revealed a number of feathery creatures resembling whole parakeet skins tied on huge hooks. Next, he not only supplied me with one of his creations, but invited me to accompany him downriver on the morrow, an offer I hastened to accept.

Thus, at misty dawn, with the ocean's incessant roar a few hundred yards away, we waded into the slick, black surface of the river with focused intent.

My bass rod handled the lure, barely. With some effort, I sent the huge fly out over the curling eddies, let it settle in, and returned it in spurts and pauses. A V-shaped wake carved toward the fly, ending in a swirl, but no strike. A grunt downstream and a burst of foam indicated that the Californian had jabbed a hook into a silver. I hastened there and observed as he handled the fish, perhaps ten pounds, then tailed it and released it for him.

Back in the upper pool, a dozen more casts brought no response, nor several dozen more. The sun was easing upward, the mist vanishing, but the salmon appeared unready for combat. California registered no more strikes, either. At length, I settled on a weathered driftwood log, eyed my fly, then opened my fly box. The biggest things within were two Reuben Woods tied on size 2 hooks, rather minuscule compared to the genuine salmon fly. After a moment's hesitation, I retired the salmon fly and tied a Rube Wood in place. Ridiculous, I realized, but what's to lose?

Back in the stream, the sunlight revealed a quartet of fish moving upcurrent a short cast away. The fly arched over the surface, settled perhaps six feet ahead of the nearest fish, and barely got its squirrel wing wet when the salmon shot forward and nailed it. Several things occurred at once. I let out horrendous yell. The fish tore off fifty yards across current, leaping four or five times in succession, then shot upstream for another fifty yards, the line peeling far down into the backing. And I became acutely aware of why salmon rods are built with extended handles. My arm, with very little leverage against this surging power, cried out for relief.

The fish went just about wherever it wished. Eventually, it rushed back toward the ocean, and I scrambled ashore, wildly sprinting down the sand past my friend, who politely reeled in as I flew past. Eventually, the salmon tired, thrashing doggedly into the shallows where the gentleman gently tailed and released it.

Five minutes and two casts later, I was on my way back downstream at full speed, past the Californian again. In what seemed like an interminable time, the earlier scenario was repeated. The fish was unhooked and released.

"What have you got on there?" the Californian squinted at my fly.

"Reuben Wood," I replied.

"Reuben Wood?"

"Yeah. A fly I use for smallmouth bass in Minnesota."

His face registered a mixture of distaste and disbelief.

This grew even more pronounced as I paraded past with numbers three, four, five and six.

"I've got another Reuben Wood," I offered. "You want to try one?" His eyes glittered as he examined my fly, but he shook his head.

Because I was playing these salmon strictly off my right arm and wrist, with no rod extension, fatigue had reached the point where I could barely cast. But I could see more salmon coursing up the current. I struggled into the stream and somehow managed a groaning, sloppy cast. Another jolting strike ensued and another streak of gleaming silver, perhaps twelve pounds, ripped off line and backing.

Not only my arm, but now my back, shoulders and neck were in extreme pain. I tried turning the rod upside down and playing the fish with my left hand, but my right could barely turn the reel. There was no earthly reason that fish stayed hooked, because it had yards of slack at various points. But, finally, fish and I drifted down to the Californian, who tailed and released it with a noted lack of enthusiasm. At this point, I ceased operations. Not only could I no longer cast, I could not raise my forearm past my belt line.

In the future another trip to Alaska is on the schedule. This time my tackle will be more adequate. And I have accumulated several genuine salmon flies at some expense. Of course, there will be a few historic, gray-squirrel Reuben Woods tucked away among the red, yellow, blue and orange feathers.

After all, you never know.

SUMMER Now I'm free

to attend to the night with all
my senses. Trees make a sheltered
little room; undersides of lush
spruce boughs bat the firelight
back down. Soft air is warm on
my face, pleasantly cool away from
the fire. Over the lake, the sky still
holds a faint memory of light.

JUDITH NIEMI
From *Night Watch In Bear Country*

Buck, Alone

ORVAL LUND

"Some keep the Sabbath by going to church ..."
EMILY DICKINSON

Out for sulfur shelf, walking up a trail, the damp gray
day muting my steps on old leaves, I see a fresh track
pressed deep into soft soil along the rock-strewn old
logging road. I stop, peer ahead hard, stand still.
The air smells rich with leafmold, the only sound
soft swish through wet-leafed trees. I walk on, quietly,
hoping wet leaves and whisper of air toward my face
keep me secret. In time, I look up from another track,
like an apostrophe mirrored, and see ahead a
gray-brown deer back up the incline, its head down
browsing, and I stop, suspecting buck from the
deep-wedged tracks I trailed. It lifts, enormous rack,
into the air, and down again to graze. It does not know
I'm there. I move closer, to peer from under a branch
spanning the trail, step on a twig, not much louder
than a leaf flapping, yet it hears, lifts and jerks its head
around and stares. I stand still, silent. Stares perhaps
five minutes, though time turns on a different fulcrum
here. Stares right at me, but doesn't seem to see,
for sure. (Have you ever been alone with God?)
Its rack's enormous, yard-stick high, covered with

velvet, odd as a candelabrum atop a head. The buck's
body, muscled, stocky, shorter than one imagines big
bucks to be, stands still, though the slightest waggle of
its head describes an arc at tips of antlers. (Angels lurk
there.) And stares. Then hunches its bulk, bolts up the
road and out of sight. I step off twenty-five to where
it stood, continue to follow, look for tracks, hope,
see no more of him. I reach the crest and find brambles
bearing blackberries — some still reddish purple, feeling
like hard nipples, not ready to eat; some so ripe they
fall into my hand. I toss a black one into my mouth,
press out its juice between tongue and palate, swallow
sweetness, spit out pith. I fill my plastic bag and
stroll on home.

Sigurd F. Olson (1899-1982) lived most of his life in Ely, Minn., first as an educator, later as a writer and conservationist. His name is

SIGURD OLSON

closely attached to the Boundary Waters Canoe Area, a wilderness his activism helped protect. Olson traveled and guided for many years in the Quetico-Superior area, and his experiences there strongly influenced him. Among many conservation achievements, he helped draft the federal Wilderness Act, signed into law in 1964 and laying out the nation's system of wilderness preservation. He wrote nine books, starting with The Singing Wilderness *in 1956, and also including* The Listening Point, The Lonely Land, Wilderness Days, *and* Reflections From the North Country. *In 1974, he received the Burroughs Medal, the highest honor in nature writing. A biography,* A Wilderness Within: The Life of Sigurd F. Olson, *was published in 1997 by the University of Minnesota Press.*

The Way of a Canoe

SIGURD OLSON

> **There is balance in the handling of a canoe, the feeling of it being a part of the bodily swing. No matter how big the waves or how the currents swirl, you are riding them as you would ride a horse, at one with their every motion.**

The movement of a canoe is like a reed in the wind. Silence is part of it, and the sounds of lapping water, bird songs, and wind in the trees. It is part of the medium through which it floats: the sky, the water, the shores.

In a canoe a man changes, and the life he has lived seems strangely remote. Time is no longer of moment, for he has become part of space and freedom. What matters is that he is heading down the misty trail of explorers and voyageurs, with a fair wind and a chance for a good camp somewhere ahead. The future is other lakes, countless rapids and the sound of them, portages through muskeg and over the ledges.

If the morning is bright and sparkling, canoes seem like birchbarks, freshly gummed for the rapids and winds ahead, and we are voyageurs, bronzed and bearded and burned from wintering in the Athabasca country. We are on our way to Grand Portage to meet old friends, to eat fresh bread again and to dance to the fiddles in the Great Hall, to fight heroic battles and do the things we can boast about for a year to come. There are songs in the wind: *"En Roulant ma boule," "La Belle Lizette,"* and *"La Claire Fontaine."* In the sound of the wind we can hear them.

The man is part of his canoe and therefore part of all it knows. The instant he dips a paddle, he flows as it flows, the canoe yielding to his slightest touch, responsive to his every whim and thought. The paddle is an extension of his arm, as his arm is part of his body. Skiing down a good slope with the snow just right comes closest, with the lightness of near-flight, the translating of even a whisper of a wish into swift action; there, too, is a sense of harmony and oneness with the earth. But to the canoeman there is nothing that compares with the joy he knows when a paddle is in his hand.

A rowboat has the fulcrum of the oarlock to control it, and the energy of a man rowing is a secondary force, but in paddling the motion is direct — the fulcrum is the lower hand and wrist, and the force is transmitted without change of direction. Because of this there is correlation and control. There is balance in the handling of a canoe, the feeling of it being a part of the bodily swing. No matter how big the waves or how the currents swirl, you are riding them as you would ride a horse, at one with their every motion.

When the point is reached where the rhythm of each stroke is as poised as the movement of the canoe itself, weariness is forgotten, and there is time to watch the sky and the shores without thought of distance or effort. At such a time the canoe glides along obedient to the slightest wish, and paddling becomes as unconscious and automatic an effort as breathing. Should you be lucky enough to be moving across a calm surface with mirrored clouds, you may have the sensation of suspension between heaven and earth, of paddling not on the water but through the skies themselves.

If the waves are rolling and you are forced to make your way against them, there is the joy of battle, each comber an enemy to be thwarted, a problem in approach and defense. A day in the teeth of a gale — dodging from island to island, fighting one's way along the lee shore of some windswept point, only to dash out again into the churning water and the full force of the wind, then do it again and again — is assurance that your sleep will be deep and your dreams profound.

One day on Namew we faced a powerful northeaster coming straight down the lake. Quartering immediately, we soon found ourselves riding against enormous rollers with broad troughs between them, the canoes coasting down one incline and up the other, almost lost in the process. Had it not been for the breadth of those intervals it would have been impossible to make headway. Attempting to pass a low, swampy island, for a long hour we barely held our own. Over and over again we battled to the hissing crests of the waves, slipped over their tops, tobogganing down the slope with enough momentum to climb the next ridge.

For a time we lost the other canoes, then saw one far to the right, a tiny silver speck miraculously making its way in the teeth of the gale. A swift glance behind and there was the third topping the crest, only to disappear in its depths. Two hours later we made the far shore, had some tea and bannock, stretched out on the flat limestone and waited for the wind to die.

There is satisfaction in reaching some point on the map in spite of wind and weather, in keeping a rendezvous with some campsite that in the morning seemed impossible of achievement. In a canoe the battle is yours and yours alone. It is your muscle and sinew, your wit and courage, against the primitive forces of the storm. That is why, when after a day of battle your tent is pitched at last in the lee of some sheltering cliff, the canoe up safe and dry, and supper under way, there is exultation that only canoemen know.

Almost as great a challenge is running with the waves down some lake where the wind has a long unbroken sweep. Riding the rollers takes more skill with a paddle; it takes an almost intuitive sense of the weight and size of them and a knowledge of how they will break behind you. A bad move may mean that a comber will wash the gunwales. A man must know not only his canoe and what it will do, but the meaning of the waves building up behind him. This is attack from the rear without a chance of looking back, a guessing at a power and lifting force he cannot see. But what a fierce joy to be riding with a thousand white-maned horses racing with the wind down some wild waterway toward the blue horizon!

It was that way on Amisk, the wind a great hand on our backs. Hissing combers were around us, and it was every canoe for itself, no chance even for a side glance to see what was happening to the others. Carefully quartering to the southeast and toward the end of a long gleaming point blood red in the sunset, I was conscious of each wave, judging its power and lift by the sharpness of the approaching hiss. If we skirted the point too close we might hit submerged rocks; if we went out too far we could be carried into the open lake with its twelve-mile sweep and miss our chance of turning into the shelter behind it.

The cliffs were still a couple of miles away. Only the tip of the point was flaming now, the base dull, angry red fading into blackness toward the west. The canoe would ride a great roller, slip off its crest, and in that moment of cascading down the slope of the trough we would start quartering. In the blow on Dead Lake the sun had been shining, the combers sparkling and alive. Now in the near-dusk they were dull and gray, the valleys in between bottomless and black. Like running a rapids in poor light, you depended on feel.

Every third or fourth wave was bigger than the rest, and I could sense its lift long before it struck. When it caught us the canoe would rise swiftly, then hurtle forward like a great spear into the spray. The cliffs were closer now, their lower parts brushed with black, only the top and very tip of the point still colored. All I could think of was a red knife sticking out into the blackness of the east, its tip alive, its blade and handle darkening into purple. We were quartering successfully and would miss the stiletto's end, but what was in its lee we did not know. Could we land there, or would we find the same precipitous cliffs we faced? We would have to camp there even if we had to climb to their tops.

Rapids, too, are a challenge. Dangerous though they may be, treacherous and always unpredictable, no one who has known the canoe trails of the north does not love their thunder and the rush of them. No man who has portaged around white water, studied the swirls, the smooth, slick sweeps and the V's that point the way above the breaks has not wondered if he should try. Rapids can be run in larger craft, in scows and rubber boats and rafts, but it is in a canoe that one really feels the river and its power.

Is there any suspense that quite compares with that moment of commitment when the canoe heads toward the lip of a long, roaring rapids and then is taken by its unseen power? At first there is no sense of speed, but suddenly you are part of it, involved in spume and spouting rocks. Then, when there is no longer any choice and a man knows that his fate is out of hand, his is a sense of fierce abandonment when all the voyageurs of the past join the rapids in their shouting.

While the canoe is in the grip of the river, a man knows what detachment means; knows that, having entered the maelstrom, he is at its mercy until it has spent its strength. When through skill or luck he has gone through the snags, the reaching rocks, and the lunging billows, he needs no other accolade but the joy that he has known.

Only fools run rapids, say the Indians, but I know this: as long as there are young men with the light of adventure in their eyes and a touch of wildness in their souls, rapids will be run. And when I hear tales of smashed canoes — and lives as well — though I join in the chorus of condemnation of the fools who take such chances, deep in my heart I understand and bid them "Bon voyage.!" I have seen what happens when food and equipment are lost far from civilization, and I know what it takes to traverse a wilderness where there are no trails but the waterways themselves. The elements of chance and danger are wonderful and frightening to experience and, though I bemoan the recklessness of youth, I wonder what the world would be like without it. I know this is wrong, but I am for the spirit that makes young men do the things they do. I am for the glory that they know.

But more than shooting white water, fighting the gales, or running before them is the knowledge that no part of any country is inaccessible where there are waterways with portages between them. The canoe gives a sense of unbounded range and freedom, unlimited movement and exploration, such as larger craft never know. Sailboats, rowboats, launches and cruisers are hobbled by their weight and size to the water on which they are placed. Not so a canoe. It is as free as the wind itself, can go wherever fancy dictates. The canoeman can camp each night in a different place, explore out-of-the-way streams and their sources, find hidden corners where no one has ever been.

Wherever there are waterways there are connecting trails between them, portages used by primitive man for countless centuries before their discovery by white men. Although overgrown and sometimes hard to find, they are always there, and when you pack your outfit across them you are one of many who have passed before. When you camp on ancient campsites, those voyageurs of the past camp with you.

The feeling of belonging to that tradition is one of the reasons canoemen love the sound of a paddle and the feel of it as it moves through the water. Long before the days of mechanized transportation, long before men learned to use the wheel, the waterways of the earth knew the dugout, the skin hunting-boat, the canoe. A man feels at home with a paddle in his hand, as natural and indigenous as with a bow or spear. When he swings through a stroke and the canoe moves forward, he sets in motion long-forgotten reflexes, stirs up ancient sensations deep within his subconscious.

When he has traveled for many days and is far from the settlements of his kind, when he looks over his cruising outfit and knows it is all he owns, that he can travel with it to a new country as he wills, he feels at last that he is down to the real business of living, that he has shed much that was unimportant and is in an old, polished groove of experience. Life for some strange reason has suddenly become simple and complete — his wants are few, his confusion and uncertainty gone, his happiness and contentment deep.

There is magic in the feel of a paddle and the movement of a canoe, a magic compounded of distance, adventure, solitude and peace. The way of a canoe is the way of the wilderness and of a freedom almost forgotten. It is an antidote to insecurity, the open door to waterways of ages past, and a way of life with profound and abiding satisfactions. When a man is part of his canoe, he is part of all that canoes have ever known.

John S. Allen was born in the tall corn country of Minnesota. Since earning a degree in biology from Winona State University, he has lived

JOHN S.
ALLEN

from Florida to Connecticut, from California to Alaska. He now lives in Minneota, Minn. As "an outdoors nut," he has walked the banks of the Mississippi from source to mouth and back, and has hiked from Mexico to Canada on both the Pacific Crest Trail and the Continental Divide Trail. As happens with most writers, "real work has occasionally reared its ugly head." John has worked on a tugboat in the Gulf of Mexico, pitched baseballs for the Army, written book reviews for an East Coast newspaper, and run a combine in Montana. He has spent the last few years giving tours of various national parks.

Listening

J O H N   S .   A L L E N

> **As I live out**
> **my time driving**
> **across the**
> **prairie — selling**
> **a tractor here,**
> **not selling a**
> **combine there —**
> **it pleases me**
> **to think of whales.**
> **Whales blowing out**
> **and breathing in.**
> **A rhythm as old as**
> **earth itself.**

My name is John. John Olson. I sell used farm machinery in little Midwestern communities. Not the most exciting job, I know. Still, it pays the bills, and now Betty is pregnant with our first child — a boy, the doctor says. Besides, I like the people. Take the two old-timers this morning. I was eating breakfast at a small cafe in southern Minnesota. Or was it northern Iowa? No matter. It was one of those places where you know, without looking, that the noon menu reads:

Beef Dinner
Beef Commercial
Beef Sandwich
Beef Vegetable Soup

Business was better than usual this morning as pheasant season was to start at noon. The cafe boomed with big, loud men from out of town. "City hunters," the locals call them in the same tone politicians are discussed. Brown-clad hunters, looking like identical loaves of bread, lined up in booths and on stools. Every hunting outfit attempted to camouflage an over-weight, out-of-shape body. Each loaf loudly looked forward to a good shoot despite rumors there weren't many birds.

Amidst all this sat two elderly men, elbow to elbow at the counter. Clean bib overalls marked them as retired farmers.

Leather faces weathered into deep seams, gnarled hands clasping coffee cups, they were extensions of land plowed since youth. To no one in particular, the old-timer on the left denounced pheasants.

"Damn fancy-colored pests. Shoulda left 'em over in China where they came from. Don't belong here on the prairie. Now you take the sage grouse. There was a bird that belonged."

"Sage grouse? Don't mean prairie chicken, do ya, old man?"

"No, goddammit! I don't! I said sage grouse and I meant sage grouse. You Johnny-come-latelies are just like pheasants — fat, slow, and born too late. They were just like regular grouse, only bigger. When I was a kid the hunters used to tell me come spring, years past, you could hear 'em drummin' all over the prairie. Called 'em sage hens like they was all females. I never heard the big drummin but I heard the last."

"The last?"

"Last! Leastwise as far as anybody knows. An' it weren't no sage hen. Last one was a male. He'd come to the ol' drummin' ground out past where the railroad waterin' tank used to be. We kids saw him every spring for five years. Winter finally got 'im, probably. Funniest damn thing, out there all by himself drummin' to nothin'."

I drove away from town picturing the old-timer's bird drumming its heart out. How far would sound echo across endless prairie? With no ears to hear, it could go on forever. It occurred as I listened that I, like the old-timer, have a private sound. When I was young, my friend Bill and I traveled some. Even spent a summer along the coast of Alaska.

It was a sunny day. Bill and I shared sandwiches as we sat on the guest lodge deck. For two farm boys, the scene could not have been more exotic. To our left, sealed behind huge plate glass windows, herds of bovine tourists ruminated lunch. To our right stretched the forests and mountains of Alaska's Fairweather Range. Practically beneath our feet lay a small cove coming off the not-too-distant ocean.

Then, the sound. "What was that?" We wheeled toward the water. At that instant, the cove exploded. A humpback whale in full body breach! I recoiled as though a hundred-pound salmon had just leaped from my bathtub. I glanced left. Hundreds of faces focused on the whale. Conversations dangled, forks dropped, lettuce fluttered to the floor. A fifty-foot animal, weighing a ton a foot, hung suspended in reflective glass. Then the crash of that giant body hitting the water. Clouds of white foam curled away. The whale was gone.

A fall night. One of my last in Alaska. Bill and I ate crab over a small beach fire. Stories of summer lasted until midnight. Then I left Bill staring into the flames and walked down the dark beach. My feet felt familiar trail; I looked back frequently, keeping a proper line on the fire. I was headed to a shell spit marking the cove's entrance. At low tide the spit stretched nearly across. I'd often gone there to listen to the ocean. I wanted to say goodbye to Alaska alone.

I rounded the small headland; the fire winked out. Night enfolded me like a monk's cloak. Several times I raised a hand in front of my face. It was as though I had no arms. No matter. My feet felt the shell-strewn spit. I walked until I could hear the gentle lap of slack water on both sides.

I sat. Nothing. No legs. No trunk. No arms. No hands. Black. A mind floating in ink. Then, the sound! Just off my right ear inside the cove. I recognized it this time. The whale was blowing. Now, to see a whale spout is to see the expected. Everyone from Herman Melville to TV insurance companies has readied us for that column of water. But take away sight and the magic arrives. The sound of the spout? A Yellowstone geyser at midnight? The sphinx clearing its throat?

But that was just the exhale. No amount of Melville or film clips could prepare one for what follows. A breath. *The* breath. I am tempted to say a whale inhaling sounds like the bellows of Jack and the Beanstalk's giant, but that simply does not have the scope. The truth is that a whale inhaling produces the most human sound on earth! It is exactly like you and me breathing in, multiplied by every human lung on earth. All of humanity inhaling at once.

For the entire night I listened to the whale blow and breathe. Incoming tide woke me. He and gray dawn must have slipped over the bar together. All my life the remembrance of that animal's steady rhythm has lent stability. As I live out my time driving across the prairie, selling a tractor here, not selling a combine there, it pleases me to think of whales. Whales blowing out and breathing in. A rhythm as old as earth itself. The oceans of the world punctured by this rhythm.

Yet, in the middle of the prairie, in the middle of the continent, I feel the rhythm weaken. I think of my whale, picture him crossing the bar, passing the shell spit, into the cove. It is just before sunset. The cove is liquid orange fire. The steady spout, a black exclamation point silhouetted against gold.

Once inside the cove, he breaches. Lodge windows stare blackly, the eyes of a skull. It is off-season, tourists and farm boys gone home. No one sees. As white foam flies, he dives deep but, after fifty, eighty, a hundred years, the great heart stutters. Perhaps it is parasites in the lungs. Possibly the marbled scar of a propeller across the base of his skull. Probably it is the loneliness of hearing his song go unanswered, amplified down watery canyons the world over. An entire planet of ocean prairie, no ears to hear.

A huge boiler with pressure valve jammed, the great heart explodes. Lungs with no air, no human bellows celebrating, the body rolls and sinks. Already small crabs are feeding. The oceans lie unbroken. Nowhere does his spout puncture the sheen. The magic of his breathing is never heard again. An entire sound has vanished from the face of the earth. He never knew, now doesn't care ... he was the last.

I can live without the sound of sage grouse. I never heard it. But life without sound of whale? Heard once, it has lived with me for twenty-five years. And what of my unborn son? Driving across the prairie, what will he listen to? Will this story be as close to fact as he ever gets? A story the real thing? The real thing a story?

Greg Breining was born in Minneapolis and, "for better or worse," has lived in Minnesota his whole life. Now he lives in St. Paul, his

GREG
BREINING

favorite Minnesota city, where he writes for a variety of magazines including Sports Illustrated, Islands, *and* International Wildlife. *His most recent books are* Minnesota *and* Return of the Eagle. *Since he learned to paddle a canoe at Boy Scout camp "a couple of centuries ago," he has floated most major streams in Minnesota and has run rivers in places as far-flung as West Virginia, Jamaica, and Java. His daughter, Kate, who appears in this story, was only a year old when she received her baptism in canoeing, tumbling over the gunwale and bobbing down the quick current of the Mississippi. "It's the last time she's fallen out of a canoe." During the last two years, Greg has kayaked more than a thousand miles around the shore of Lake Superior to research a book on the world's largest lake.*

True North Woods

GREG BREINING

" Portages here are gauged in rods, a logging measure that equals sixteen and a half feet. This portage measures four hundred eighty rods. Having walked down nearly three dozen portage trails, I no longer have to run through the mathematics. I have thoroughly internalized the rod as a unit of measurement. "

From the first, Kate's pack had given us trouble. It was one of mine. We tried it on at home, loaded with thirty pounds of gear, nearly half her own weight. It sagged on her shoulders, and the belt encircled her skinny waist like a ring around Saturn. Some angular part of the payload gouged her back. The hike down the driveway and back seemed to stagger her.

So now, it is with some trepidation that my nine-year-old daughter steps from the canoe to begin her first portage — a very short portage — of our three-day trip through the Boundary Waters Canoe Area. I feel the same concern. I want Kate to take part in portaging, that is, carrying canoe and camping gear from lake to lake, a necessary ritual of traveling these waterways. At the same time, I want her to enjoy herself. I've saved the heaviest items for my own pack, leaving Kate with soft, bulky gear that will rest easy on her back. I hold her pack as she slides her thin arms into the straps.

"Stop and rest whenever you want," I say.

"I will," she replies, mildly reassured.

Then I watch her set out down the well-worn path. I shoulder my own pack and the canoe and follow her into the dark shadows of the woods.

Kate has canoed with me since she was seven months old. She was a year and a half when we took our first long outing, a three-day trip down the Mississippi. Since then we have spent many days on the water, but never have we paddled and camped together in an area as remote as this. I don't doubt Kate will take to the paddling and camping. She'll even tolerate the mosquitoes. No, my main concern is with the portages, which range from a few feet to more than a mile. True, we could put in on a big lake, like Basswood, Saganaga or Brule, where dozens of islands and many miles of water would give us plenty to explore. But I want to give Kate the true Northwoods experience. And that means following the portage trails deep into the wilderness.

My worries evaporate once I reach the end of the portage. Kate stands smiling by the next lake, waiting for me to load her pack into the canoe. "I didn't get sore at all," she says brightly. "It was pretty easy." We load the canoe, Kate jumps into the bow seat, and we push off onto a long, island-studded lake rimmed by rocky shore.

The Boundary Waters is a land of 1.1 million acres of forest and some 2,500 lakes. It is a place where loons call and wolves howl. With few exceptions, it is a land where motors are not allowed, and progress is measured by the firm bite of a paddle in clear water and the weight of a canoe and pack on your shoulders. It is a natural place for kids, with freedom to hike, canoe, swim, fish and explore, following the trails used by Ojibwa Indians and French Canadian voyageurs hundreds of years ago. The challenge is to get kids involved in the paddling, portaging, and routine chores of camping while keeping the trip easy enough — for parent and child — to be fun. That requires being prepared and knowing how to make adjustments in your plans.

After our portage, Kate and I face a long paddle across the lake. Here I know Kate will excel. She seems to love the feel of the paddle and the quiet glide of the hull through the water.

We stop on an island for a quick lunch of pita bread, cheese and sausage. I spread our map across my knees for Kate to see. We trace our route so far — down the light blue fetch of Sawbill Lake, across the black dotted lines of our first portage, and across Alton Lake to the red dot representing the island campsite where we now sit.

After lunch we make two more portages, longer than the first. The second is nearly a mile. But we are in no hurry, and we rest when we need to. Kate pronounces the last carry "horrible," but I can tell by her spirit and the spring in her step that it's not so bad. In taking the last portage we seem to have left behind most other canoeists. We are alone on Grace Lake, a mirror of reddening sky cut by the sharp bow of our canoe. We pick a campsite on a rocky point that slopes into the lake.

Kate leaps to the tasks at hand. She helps unload the canoe and carry gear up from shore. Together we pick a tent site, set the tent, and spread out sleeping pads and bags. As I start dinner, Kate forages for clusters of ripe blueberries. My Boundary Waters dinners have common themes: simple, cheap, and lightweight. Tonight we cook rice pilaf (using water drawn from the middle of the lake, where it is clearest), stir-fried with a little olive oil, garlic, cubed sausage and green pepper. Kate, never a picky eater, cleans her plate and takes seconds. After dinner, we take the canoe on the lake to fish. We hook two small bass but then lay down the rods. We paddle lazily around a cluster of islands. Kate climbs out and claims one as her own — a rocky bump the size of a car, populated by a couple of yard-high spruce and some leathery-leafed shrubs.

Low clouds settle in. Gray sky, gray water, hills of dark green spruce. The scene makes me ache with a melancholy I can't identify. I feel as though I sit on the cold, hard heart of the continent. The Ojibwa Indians saw spirits in every rock, wave and tree. I first came to this country when I was twelve, on a canoe trip with my dad and younger brother. Floating on this lake with Kate, I feel the company of other spirits.

When I first traveled the Boundary Waters with my dad and brother, we paddled and portaged across several lakes before setting camp, much as Kate and I have done. We spent the next three days canoeing, fishing, searching for turtles and beavers along shore, hiking the portage trails, cooking, and lounging about camp.

"We could do the same thing," I tell Kate over breakfast. As I study the map, she munches a strawberry Pop Tart. "We can stay on this lake and take short trips into other lakes today and tomorrow," I say. "We can swim and fish and paddle during the day and camp here at night. Or we can do a loop."

A loop. Kate seems to come fully awake with this information. A loop! Why sit still when you can be on the move, ready to see something completely different?

"A loop!" she says without hesitation. "Let's do a loop!"

I trace the route on the map: Northwest through a chain of a half-dozen lakes and scattered unnamed ponds and more than a dozen portages. Then east along something called the Louse River. From there, we would puddle jump through a knot of lakes, ponds and portages back to our starting point. In all, about thirty-five miles and thirty-five portages, including a monster carry of a mile and a half near the end. The problem is this: If we get tired halfway through, we have to finish the loop, or retrace our route, to get home. Still, we have three days, and enough food to stay out an extra day if we need to.

"It might be a lot of work," I say.

"Let's do it."

"Okay. If we make Polly Lake by this afternoon, we'll do the loop. If we don't, we stay the night, turn around and come back."

We strike camp, load packs into the canoe, don life vests, and push out onto Grace Lake, putting our paddles to the water.

The Boundary Waters has been a thoroughfare for hundreds of years. Ojibwa Indians had established a network of water routes and portage trails that lead from Lake Superior, through the Boundary Waters, deep into the heart of Canada. During the late 1700s and early 1800s, French Canadian voyageurs followed the chain of lakes, carrying pots, axes and other barter goods to Indian trappers in the interior, and returning to the Great Lakes, and eventually Montreal, with valuable beaver pelts.

Sitting six to ten in twenty-five-foot birchbark canoes, the voyageurs sang as they paddled, and carried at least two ninety-pound packs on the portages. In 1826, Thomas McKenney accompanied a group of voyageurs who traveled seventy-nine miles in a single day. From dawn to dark, McKenney calculated, each voyageur put his paddle to the water 57,600 times. "No human beings, except the Canadian French, could stand this," he wrote.

Kate and I have no intention of matching that pace, though with a day's practice under our belts, we paddle and portage with pleasing efficiency. As the canoe glides toward the landing, I step into the shallow water with my rubber boots to protect the lightweight hull from rocks. I help Kate to shore, hold her pack, and watch as she disappears down the trail. I stow our two paddles and the spare in the stern of the canoe, secure them with a bungee cord, tuck the map in the pocket of the pack, and sling the pack onto my back. Then, making sure my footing is solid, I lift the canoe, cradle it in the crook of my arm, and swing it overhead until it rests comfortably on my shoulders. Then I, too, set off down the path — no loose ends, nothing left behind. As much as anything in the Boundary Waters, I enjoy this efficiency of travel, the existential ease of moving through the country like a salmon upriver or a vagabond on the highway. But what I remember most is the sight of Kate's blue pack bouncing through the green woods, as her long, springy legs stride down the portage trail.

We reach Polly Lake by early afternoon. It is clear we can make our loop with time to spare. So we slow down, drifting when the wind is with us and savoring the sights of this wilderness. We peer into the suggestive depths to a rock point or sunken log far beneath the surface. On portage trails we take note of the holiday colors of bright red bunchberry and stop occasionally to identify flowers and munch blueberries. On a little creek we glide silently in anticipation of a moose. The moose fails us, so we drift along the boggy margins of the stream, a quivering mat of sphagnum, so infertile in this rock-ribbed environment that even the plants look for supplemental nutrition and have turned carnivorous. We touch the sticky leaves of tiny sundews, which snare flying insects, and poke our fingers into the watery traps of pitcher plants.

Clouds gather through the afternoon. A thunderstorm catches us on the portage to Malberg Lake. Drenched, we begin to search for a campsite. The first we find is second-rate, low and marshy. The next several are taken by other canoeists. Finally, we paddle into a back bay just as another canoe emerges, occupied by three young men in rain gear. That can only mean that the site is already claimed, by them or someone else.

"Is that campsite taken?" I ask without much hope.

"Yeah, by a big black bear," one man says. I laugh. "We're not kidding."

I've run into bears many times in the Boundary Waters. They can be relentless in their quest for food, and they have always frightened me a bit — too many *Outdoor Life* "true adventures" and tall tales from my dad.

"Let's go somewhere else," I say to Kate.

"Can we see the bear? " she asks. Her curiosity and lack of fear surprise me.

"Okay."

The site comes into view. No bear. No campers either. Should we camp? Why not? These are black bears, not grizzlies. For that matter, the bear could be headed toward any campsite on the lake by now. Besides, it's getting late, and Malberg Lake, the nexus of other canoe routes coming in from the west and north, is filling with canoeists. So we set up camp. We pitch the tent and spread our sleeping pads and bags inside. Then we paddle out into the lake to dip a big cooking pot for drinking water. When we turn the canoe toward shore, the bear stands on a broad outcrop, about a hundred feet from camp.

"Paddle hard," I tell Kate. We speed toward the bear and begin to yell. The bear runs off a few feet. It turns, sees that we are still coming, and flees into the brush. At the very least, I want the bear to think twice about coming back.

Kate carries water and stirs pasta. Dinner that night is pasta parmesan, eaten as we look over our shoulders at the dark woods behind. We wash the dishes scrupulously and patrol the site for crumbs that would give the bear a reason to visit camp. We stash the garbage in a backpack with our food. Using a hundred-foot length of strong rope, I suspend the pack between two widely spaced trees, a full fifteen feet off the ground. I stack the pots and pans by the fire grate. We build a fire. Thick smoke rolls from the wet wood, barely rising in the damp air. We drink cocoa until dark, talking about school, sports, travel, places we've seen and haven't seen. Then we go to bed. Through the night I hear noises. Surely a mouse, I tell myself. Too noisy for a bear, which can pad through the forest with surprising stealth.

Suddenly the pots and pans scatter. I shout and think I hear the bear run off. Kate stirs groggily. "Don't worry, honey, he's gone." She seems unconcerned and returns to sleep. I try, too. After all, what's to worry about? The bear will do no harm, unless he figures a way to cut the rope and steal the pack out of the trees. And if he's capable of that, he's more bear than I care to deal with.

We hear no more of the bear and eat breakfast in peace. We strike camp, scud to the west like the low gray clouds, and enter the Louse River. It is like a thousand other small waterways in the Boundary Waters — pretty in its own way, especially to a moose or beaver, but aimless, without ambition. I study the grassy weeds lying on the surface of the creek. They point generally back the way we came, toward Malberg Lake. We must be going upstream. In places the channel is so choked with water lilies that we must pole our way through to open water. Occasionally a tributary branches to one side. When you're headed clearly down a river, it's impossible to get lost; the current unfailingly takes you where it will. But when you paddle up a river, especially one as phlegmatic as the Louse, it is possible to head off on a fork to parts unknown. So at any puzzling intersection, Kate and I consult our map before pressing on.

Shallow rocky stretches occasionally block the stream. We portage. As day wears on, the portage trails grow fainter.

Forest Service work crews normally clear out deadfalls, but it's clear the Louse hasn't seen a chain saw in ages. Finally, it happens. A portage appears where it doesn't belong. Is our map in error? Or am I? Have I simply lost track? Or, worse, have we strayed off onto a different route? It is amazing how easily panic rises, how quickly you think of spending the night in the woods, location unknown, hacking out a makeshift camp in a stand of birch and balsam.

"Are we lost, Dad?"

Still, we had food, tent, sleeping bags and canoe. How uncomfortable could it be? Just press on, press on. Soon you'll come to a lake that you can recognize, a landmark that will bring the map back into focus.

"A little, but we'll find our way."

And so we do. After two portages, the Louse River gives way to a wide stretch of blue. It can only be Bug Lake. The name notwithstanding, it is a relief from the claustrophobia of what Kate and I have dubbed "the accursed Louse." The clouds give way to sun, as though the universe has shown us the way. We pull our canoe onto an outcrop, grab the food, and climb a high overlook to survey the lake as we eat. We scan the map with the comforting knowledge that we know where we are.

Kate and I spend the fat of the afternoon hopping from one small lake to another, slipping once again into the comfortable groove of canoe travel. We see no one else most of the day. The reason is clear enough: Behind us lies the accursed Louse. Ahead, sealing off the other end of the chain of lakes we follow, is The Portage.

Portages here are gauged in rods, a logging measure that equals sixteen and a half feet. The Portage measures four hundred eighty rods. Having walked down nearly three dozen portage trails, I no longer have to run through the mathematics. I have thoroughly internalized the rod as a unit of measurement. After three days, I know how long it is, how it feels in the knees, in the thighs, along the neck where the pack straps and carrying yoke cramp your shoulders. Four hundred eighty rods is exactly a mile and a half.

I have tried to ready Kate for this by telling her we have the rest of the afternoon to take this portage, if necessary. We can rest as many times as we want. She, in turn, regards The Portage with bouts of giddy anticipation and melodramatic dread.

"Oh, no!" she cries as we glide to the landing. "The Portage!" But she's smiling. I help her with her pack.

"If you get tired, or if you're not sure of the way, just wait for me," I tell her. Then Kate, true to form, disappears down the trail before I can shoulder my load.

The trail rises from the lake, then levels. I try to turn my attention from the load on my back. I watch the forest floor for flowers, berries, and other small treasures. Suddenly I come to a stretch of mud. Then another. Finally, a long black quagmire. No sign of Kate. She apparently found a way around. Or through. I take a step along the edge. Instantly I sink to my knee. I try another step and hear a great sucking sound. It's my boot, buried deep in muck. I'm left standing on one leg like a giant flamingo, with only a sock on one foot and a hundred pounds of pack and canoe on my back. I throw down my load in disgust and dig through the mud for my boot. I finally catch up to Kate at a fork in the path.

"I didn't know which way to go," she says. We drop our gear and follow the left fork down to a swamp creek.

"We can carry our stuff down here and try paddling," I tell her. "But we may have to portage again a little ways ahead. Or we can take the other path and take the portage all at once."

"I want to take the whole thing," Kate says resolutely. "I want to take the four-eighty." I've created a monster.

We portage on. The trail rises and travels along higher ground. Finally it begins to drop, and I spot the refreshing blue of water through the dark trees. At water's edge, Kate has shed her pack and happily munches M&Ms and sunflower seeds. Her boots are caked with muck.

"What did you think?" I ask.

"Not bad."

"What was the worst part?"

"The mud."

We load and launch. As the canoe glides along, the little swamp river gradually widens and grows into a long, rocky lake. We enjoy the remainder of the day, the clear fetch of water, open view, and light-filled sky. We have just one more portage of thirteen rods. After that, nothing but the open highway. This place thrills me, and so does my daughter.

Sam Cook grew up in Kansas, but was lured north in 1976. He has never left. He and Phyllis, his wife and canoe-paddling partner,

SAM COOK

lived for a time in Ely, Minn., on the fringes of the Quetico-Superior canoe region. They later settled in Duluth.

Sam is the outdoors writer for the Duluth News-Tribune *and one of the most popular newspaper writers in his area of the country. His books include three collections of essays,* Up North, CampSights *and* Quiet Magic, *and a humorous title,* If This Is Mid-Life, Where's the Crisis? *All were published by Pfeifer-Hamilton of Duluth. A new collection of Sam's outdoor essays is due out in 1998.*

The Trout Fisherman

SAM COOK

> **The old man was sitting on a cedar log that hung out over a ledge. He was literally part of the river. As he sat there, the water flowed under and on both sides of him. Both his feet were in the water. His worm was in the pool.**

At first it had looked like a trail, not a worn path, but a meandering opening among the thimbleberries. The trail dissolved into the forest, but that didn't bother Enok Olson. Now he was coursing randomly through the aspen and large-leafed aster, stepping over deadfalls, and batting branches away from his face. It didn't seem that he was trying to find the stream so much as he was being drawn to it. Perhaps that's the way it is when you're almost eighty-nine and brook trout streams have been drawing you to their banks for half a century.

Olson pulled up and leaned against an aspen. His entourage, Lloyd Gilbertson and I, found our own leaning trees and caught our breath.

"This is tough," Olson said.

It was tough, tougher than the brook trout fishing Olson does closer to his cabin home near Silver Bay, Minnesota. There a neighbor woman drops him off at a bridge on a nearby river and returns to pick him up later in the day.

We were a few miles up the Gunflint Trail north of Grand Marais, crashing through the brush, seeking a stream Olson hadn't fished since he was, oh, probably eighty-three. The stream has a name, of course, but it won't be used here.

"It would be better if you didn't mention it," Olson had said.

It isn't that he wants to keep the fishing for himself. He will likely never set his hip boot in this stream again after this visit. But Olson is a trout fisherman. It's the principle of the thing.

Soon we were wandering again, Olson out in front with his fly rod in one hand and his walking stick in the other. He moved along steadily, past the rose hips and alders and balsams. Watching Olson up ahead was like seeing the cover of a 1920 L.L. Bean catalog coming to life. He wore an old gray fishing cap and an ancient fishing coat whose corduroy collar was frayed from years of rubbing against a whiskered neck. The coat, of heavy cotton duck, was originally brown, but the years and the North Shore weather had mellowed it to a gentle buff.

Olson's khaki pants disappeared at knee level into his turned-down hip boots. The boots, too, showed the years. Patches were covered with more patches, and the felt that Olson had glued on the soles was all but gone. His walking stick was an alder, waist-high and stout. His fiberglass fly rod bore the scars of many treks like this one. Its varnish was scratched, and a couple of its guides were bent.

It was the creel, more than anything else, that gave Olson's outfit its character. A classic creel like Olson's is a wicker basket that trout anglers put their fish in. Olson's hung from one shoulder and rested against his hip as if it were part of him. "It's forty years old," he said. "I used to get these from Michigan Willow for three or four dollars. Now I couldn't buy one for fifty dollars." The bottom of the creel had long since broken out, the victim of too many riverside slips and falls. Olson had patched it with the tin of some old coffee cans, the tin held in place by pieces of wire woven through the wicker.

On we went. The terrain began to drop, though the trout stream was nowhere in sight. Soon the descent was so steep we had to walk sideways to maintain our footing. Olson clutched at branches and grabbed onto birch trunks, using his arms to help his legs.

"I just wish I was about twenty years younger," he said.

Olson's companions let the remark sink in. One couldn't help but wonder when even a sixty-nine-year-old had last clambered down this hill.

———————————

Soon we could hear the stream, and finally, after sliding part of the way on our rear ends and climbing through some cedars, we were there. At one of our pauses on the way down, Olson had said, "We may not get any fish, but I know you're gonna marvel when you see that river." He was right. This wasn't just a stream. It was a canyon. Sheer walls of sedimentary rock rose from the water's edge, some forty feet high. Where there were no walls, the valley rose at a pitch like the one we had just slid down. The water was low, almost as low as Olson ever remembered seeing it. It was the color of weak tea in the shallows, but coffee brown in the pools below ledges and along those sheer walls.

Olson couldn't wait to get a worm on his hook and get it in the water. He wasn't asking for much. "If I get one fish, I'm happy," he said. "If I get two, I'm really happy." He pulled his hip boots up, put his walking stick in front of him, and waded into the stream. It's hard to imagine what it must be like to fish a stream at eighty-nine, when your eyes won't see all you want them to see and your wading legs aren't as steady as they once were.

"I can't see the hook, so I gotta go by feel when I put a worm on," Olson said. His feel was good. He had a worm on in no time and flipped it into a pool of fast water below a ledge.

"The fish could be in there, but I don't think so," he said. Walking stick clamped under one arm, he played out line. Suddenly he raised his rod tip, the line tightened, and a fish was dancing on the surface of the pool.

"He's got one!" Gilbertson hollered.

He had one, all right. Olson dropped his walking stick and began working line in. A broad grin spread across his face. He had made it back to his river. He had caught a fish. He was a happy man. But he hadn't landed his fish yet. He picked up his walking stick and, keeping his line tight, shuffled over to the far shore. He tossed the stick behind him and reached into his fishing coat. From an inside pocket, he pulled out a landing net, the collapsible kind, with a rim of flexible metal that sprang into a full hoop when it was released. Olson popped the net open, stooped over the water, and pulled his fish close. It was a small brook trout, but nice by inland stream standards. Olson drew it along the surface until it was over the landing net. Then he scooped the brookie up and rose to his feet, beaming.

Hands shaking ever so slightly, he felt for the hook, found it, and pulled it free. Holding on to the fish with his whole hand, he slipped it into the creel. As Olson refolded the net and stuck it back in his jacket, Gilbertson asked him a question. "How many trout have you caught now, Enok?"

Olson thought for a moment. "Well, this year, I'm probably in the fifties," he said.

"No, I mean always."

"Oh, for heaven's sake."

Olson, one of nine children, was born in southern Sweden in 1895. He and Esther, his wife of sixty-one years, came to the United States as newlyweds in 1923. They could speak no English, but it wasn't long before Enok, an electrician, hooked up with Minnesota Power, where he worked for the next thirty-seven years. During those years, Enok and Esther went to the woods as often as they could.

"Esther would have all of our things ready on Friday evening," Enok said. "If I'd get home at five-thirty, we'd be ready to go by six." They fished almost all of the North Shore streams, crashing into backcountry and making camps in the middle of nowhere. Their love of the North Shore led them to build a modest cabin three miles east of Silver Bay. They retired there in 1960, and live there still on what is now called the Olson Road.

Someone asked Enok whether the road was named after him.

"I like this," he said. "There's the Lincoln Memorial, the Washington Monument, and the Olson Road. All the important people have something named after them."

———————————————

Enok's days usually start about four in the morning, when he and Esther wake up. A typical breakfast is the one he had before this week's fishing trip: fried potatoes, pickled herring, a hard-boiled egg, and coffee. He loves to work with wood in his shop. He makes oversized wooden cribbage boards, "for the old people."

Spend a day on the river with Enok and you will come to know a gentle yet spunky man. You'll hear about the deer he shot on opening day of deer season in 1941, the day he became a U.S. citizen, his first day on the job in America. And you'll hear fishing stories. Many involve his brother — or "brudder" as he pronounces it — also quite a trout fisherman.

"I found this stream, and it was a good one," he said. "I'd been fishing it for quite a while, and I always caught fish. I never told my brudder about it. Finally, I told him, 'OK, I'll take you there.' So one day I take him. We get in there, and he says, 'Oh, I been fishing this spot for a long time.'"

Enok isn't given to exaggeration, even when it comes to fishing. "I wouldn't lie a half-inch about the size of a trout," he said. "But if someone asks me, 'Where'd you get all those nice trout?' I'll lie like an SOB."

If you spend that day with Enok, you will also come to understand a little about being old. Enok knows. He's had more experience at it than most people.

"Don't think it's miserable being old," he will say. He became a member of the North Shore Golden Age Club in Silver Bay. He liked the club, but wanted to change its name. "I wanted to call it the North Shore Senior Citizens Club," he said. "It isn't the Golden Age. The first year after you retire, it's the Golden Age. After that, it gets tough."

———————————— ✒ ————————————

It was midday on the river. Olson had worked upstream from the pool where he caught his first fish, looking for a hole he remembered. He would sit there, he said. Gilbertson and I fished downstream. We caught and kept about ten trout, releasing many more. None were big — ten inches tops — but they were electric with fight. Then we headed back to find our partner. We came around one of the river's precipitous bends, and there he was. He had found his hole. He was sitting on a cedar log that hung out over a ledge. The stream ran wide and shallow over the ledge, then dropped three or four feet into one of the finest looking holes a trout fisherman would ever want to see.

Olson was literally part of the river. As he sat there, the water flowed under and on both sides of him. Both his feet were in the water. His worm was in the pool. We walked on up to see him.

"I've caught three fish," he said. "Did you catch anything?"

We told him we'd caught brookies, rainbows, and one brown. He seemed even happier about our luck than he was about the three brookies lying on damp cedar boughs in that patched creel of his. And remember, one would have made him happy. While Gilbertson and I cooked trout on a stick over a tiny fire, Olson talked. His blue eyes danced like the river before him as he told of bygone fishing trips. We ate fish and licked fingers and listened to the river.

———————————— ✒ ————————————

The climb out of the canyon was a workout. Nine times we stopped to rest.

"The doc says my ticker's good, so I don't worry about that," Olson said. That was good to hear. He was probably the only one among us who wasn't worried about that ticker. On we climbed.

"I think the hill's steeper than it used to be," Olson said.

We stopped to rest again.

"I won't say it yet, but when we get to the top, I'll say it was a damn nice trip."

Up we went, and up. Occasionally, Olson would grab a birch tree and Gilbertson, six-foot-five, two hundred thirty pounds, would give him a shove. But almost every step out of that valley was Olson's own. It was simply a matter of time.

Finally we reached the top of the ridge and followed a trail to a pasture. From there it was a quarter-mile walk to our car. Because the sun was hot, we took it slowly. When we turned down a lane and saw the car, Olson spoke.

"Is it all right to say I made it now?"

"You made it, Enok," Gilbertson said.

"Well, I wasn't too damn sure I would, either."

Olson had returned to his river. He had found his way in there, caught some fish, and made the climb out. A fellow couldn't help recalling something Olson had said, sitting there by the stream eating lunch. The water was cascading into that pool and three trout were lying in the creel and the smoke from the fire smelled like every fire ever built beside a stream.

"I'm glad I had a chance to fish this one more time," he said. "It's beautiful."

He knew — he had to know — that he wouldn't be coming back again, not to the canyon. But he had shared his river with a couple of youngsters who knew what it meant to him. They will go back, and when they do, Enok Olson will always be with them.

Judith Niemi is the director of Women in the Wilderness, based in St. Paul, Minnesota. For twenty years she has taught outdoor skills

JUDITH NIEMI

and guided women's wilderness trips, traveling in the Arctic and the Amazon as well as in her home country, northern Minnesota. *She believes canoeing is one of the finest pursuits in life, and also enjoys wild ricing, berry picking and sometimes teaching wilderness and travel literature. Her writings include* Rivers Running Free: a Century of Women's Canoe Adventures *(co-edited with Barbara Wieser),* The Basic Essentials of Women Outdoors, *and many essays.*

Night Watch in Bear Country

JUDITH NIEMI

> **Another version of The Fall: Humans and animals violated the original covenant, and the Great Spirit scrambled our languages. Makwa is the animal who is believed still most tuned to human speech; he should not be spoken of rudely.**

We build up the driftwood fire to last all night; its clear flames work slowly into a big silver log. We haul every last crumb of food to the metal bear locker, a five-minute walk down the beach and then a nervous couple of minutes into the darkening woods. We circle our tents around the fire and volunteer for nightwatch. Excessive, I think. A tad paranoid — but we have reason to be jumpy.

Always before, four previous trips, we've found the bears on this remote Canadian shore of Lake Superior to be mannerly wild creatures, a benign and elusive presence. They scampered away when we canoed by. Occasionally they wandered near camp at night, but took only a look around, left only footprints. In the morning we'd follow the easy-going, pigeon-toed trail as it moseyed along the beach. This year, something has changed in Pukaskwa National Park; this is the third place where a casually fearless bear has rummaged around in our gear, or chased us out of a good campsite.

Earlier this evening, long before dark, a small bear strolled right into an empty tent. He broke a tent pole, not aggressively, just in bulky, bearish unconcern. He dragged off a pack full of clothes, left souvenir tooth holes in a T-shirt and swimming suit, made off with a wallet. Of course it could be *she*. We really don't know, but a party of women finds it easier to attribute this bumptious behavior to a young male, a teenage hood. We got all the loot back, but as Janice said, re-pocketing her wallet, a bear loose with credit cards — now *that's* scary. So once again we post an all-night guard.

After the last bear chase, around midnight, I catch a nap. An hour later, someone whispers my name and hands me her fire-poking stick, a ceremonial transfer of authority. Shift One shuffles off to bed and Joan and I settle silently around the fire. I get out a pen and notebook; soon my companion is dozing.

The bear is snoozing too, I'll just bet on it. Like our previous bear, miles down the shore, he'll show up again for breakfast. Our fear makes us imagine bears as nocturnal, but they really aren't, except to avoid people, and this one has no objection to our company. Snug in his glossy black fur, he's probably taking his ease right now, bedded in soft sphagnum moss under a thatch of spruce so dense we wouldn't notice him from ten feet away. He's snoring peacefully, while I lose sleep, listening.

Since listening is my job, I spend a long while sorting out the night noises. Lake Superior, calm for once, sloshes gently on the sandy shore. A sharper sound, like water on cobblestones, is little waves curling over. From behind me in the forest come small snaps and clicks, more water sounds bouncing off the cliff face, a confusing ventriloquial effect. This afternoon, we heard a light tapping back there. "A hermit!" we said. "It's an old-timer re-roofing his secret trapping cabin." But, as we'd suspected, it proved to be a bear diligently scuffing at the frustrating bear box. There's no tapping now. An occasional loud bonk could be read as a kayak being flipped over, but is only the surf. Over all the lake's conversations with itself and with its shores float a few other small noises — fire snaps, soft snoring, a high, thin ringing in my ears, so subtle I rarely notice it except at times of intense listening. I can't decide if it's just my aging ears or something metaphysical out there trying to get my attention.

Once I've cataloged all these background sounds, I relax. If the bear does come, I'll trust my ears to catch the new noise — a metallic click of pots hanging on the trip wires we've strung across the paths, or the brushing of a sturdy body through the trees. I'm free now to attend to the night's beauty. Soft night air is warm on my face, pleasantly cool away from the fire. The undersides of lush spruce boughs bat the firelight back down, making our fire circle a snug little room, open only on the lake side, where water and sky still hold a faint memory of light. Over the mouth of the Willow River, a planet glows, Venus, I guess. Overhead the Big Dipper, or Great Bear, fills the sky.

The fire burns low, so I push two pieces of wood farther in, nudging them into perfect aesthetically pleasing alignment. I wonder just why we built the fire.

"So, is it true that animals instinctively fear fire?" Louise had asked me earlier, as we collected our night's wood supply.

"Nah. I doubt it."

Our bear could hardly keep himself from joining us around the fire. We wolfed down our chocolate mousse in unseemly haste, trying to pretend it showed panache to eat dessert with a bear watching. Even when all the food was gone, even with seven of us shouting unwelcome, he kept circling like a dog forbidden to come to the table. His small, expressive eyes peered wistfully from the shadows; he came tiptoeing up behind our woodpile.

"No," I admitted, "I guess it's just that we'd be intimidated without fire."

Without the fire to tend, what would I be doing now? Sitting in the dark, hyperalert to every sound, straining my weak senses of hearing and smell, frustrated by lack of night vision? I'd be tense and edgy. Or maybe my mind and spirit would go wandering more freely into the dark space all around. We like to think fires encourage dreaming, but a campfire also limits us. It provides a hypnotic point of concentration and keeps us comfortably fixed in the familiar world, the visible. Our attention stays in a small circle, on our own warm bodies and minds, on things we can do: gather wood, poke the fire higher, cozy up our world.

Reluctance to give up campfires isn't just nostalgia. We like to imagine some ancestral memory of sheltering from dire wolf, saber-tooth tiger, or cave bear. More likely, fire keeps us safe from something in ourselves, from the part of us that really wants to be with the bear. What could I learn to see, or feel, if I let myself get friendly with the dark?

———————————————

That first bear startled me and changed the trip. At this latitude in June, twilight lasts until after eleven. Most people had gone to bed. Enjoying the purple dusk, tucking things in, I stumbled over our plastic food barrel where it shouldn't be, and heard a sharp, businesslike growl of warning. Dark eyes stared at me from the underbrush. I scrambled backward, fast. Something scuffled in a jack pine. Bark showered down.

Then, in the growing dark, the bear, or maybe bears, seemed to be everywhere, sitting on Janice's tent, standing in mine, overhead in the trees, rooting around in our boats. Confused, nervous, shrilling our whistles, we tried to get organized. Some of us lugged away the heavy food packs with the real prizes like cheese and sausage and butter; the others covered us, brandishing sticks like lion tamers. A huge bear reached into our unguarded canoe and went rollicking off triumphantly with a red stuff sack. Not a big prize, just the condiments. No one suggested following.

In the morning, the bear came again, just one, and we gradually concluded we'd had only one visitor, a small one at that. I probably outweighed it; if it walked up to me, which seemed likely, its shoulders wouldn't reach my waist. A yearling, we thought, so thin its ribs showed under a dull, dry coat. Long, scruffy hair stood up on its neck, a kind of punk cut. On one side was a reddish patch. A marked bear? A known troublemaker? Maybe just mange. His tracks in the sand were small, the size of my own hand, fingers curled.

Daylight made us bolder in bear chasing, but no more successful.

"Git out git out scram! Go home!"

"He is home. That's the trouble."

"Hey, go make an honest living. Be a real bear."

We tried profanity, shrill nagging, a gym teacher's no-nonsense voice. We blew whistles, banged pots, barked like terriers. None of it worked. The bear roamed our beach looking melancholy, preoccupied. It paid little attention to us as we packed up, but strolled right up to the canoes and kayaks as we hastily launched.

Now, after several bear visits, I sit listening for bears, and wondering: What should our attitude and actions be toward them? They are just black bears, rarely aggressive. Our visitors are young animals, engaging in behavior that's of slight danger to us, although a lot of potential danger to them. We have empathy. It's been a cold, late spring; until berry season, still weeks away, the most high-calorie food a bear could find is what we've brought.

As we paddled away from that scrawny bear standing on the shore, Jesse said, "I've been thinking a lot about overfed campers and starving bears." A research biologist, she's thinking large scale, of humans selfishly altering good habitat for our own purposes, of how our visit could endanger the bears, who learn so quickly. We've been telling each other bear stories, of course, and someone remembered the bear in the Great Smokies who one glorious day found Kentucky Fried in a Volkswagen, and for many years after made a habit of peeling open VW beetles.

So it is both self-interest and our duty to protect our chocolate mousse, to yell and scream and create "aversive encounters." Still, it seems rude to shout profanity or insults, and I don't like it. There's such ambiguity: This credit-card-carrying bear is definitely a pain, but he represents the wildness we're looking for. He's a clown, an unpredictable creature of impressive strength, and an intelligent being whose clan has evoked awe as well as fear from my species.

In fact, we did have a respectful understanding with a bear a few days ago, at least I believe we did. The scrawny bear followed us, taking the backpackers' trail down the shore. He turned up at our campsite at dawn, waking us with a mighty rustle of plastic, pawing through our spare clothing. Finding nothing of interest, he climbed a tree supporting the too-short bear pole and batted down the little sack we'd slung up there last thing before bed: snack food, toothpaste, soap. Well, actually, a couple of women admitted, their whole toilet kits.

"So what did you lose that matters?"

"Thyroid medication. I'll do OK without."

"Antidepressants."

"My high blood pressure medicine."

"Oh, damn. Let's go find that stuff. "

Not far away we found the bear lounging on the moss, lying on his little treasure-hoard. Though he looked so underfed, he wasn't tearing into the bags but savoring each bite. With dainty gestures, he poked around with his long nose, licking up one peanut, one M&M at a time, with the patience he'd use extracting ants from a log. Several yards behind him lay a pile of shredded plastic bags, brown vials, a plastic seven-day pill case.

Slowly I edged toward the mess, not sneaking, just easing in, measuring the distance and the bear's mood.

"Hey, good morning, makwa." I was faking a calm voice and borrowing a name from the local people, the *anishinabeg*, or Ojibwe, who generally have a more respectful relationship with bears than my own tribe. "Makwa, I'm not taking anything you want. It might harm you. We need these things." I didn't feel bold, exactly, just a little high, totally alert. It was a performance; I tried to make a connection to my listener.

Makwa shuffled nervously and raised his shoulders. "Careful!" hissed someone behind me. But the bear only rotated his cupped ears in my direction and turned back to snacking. I kept murmuring and edged closer. With a long stick I reached things out of the trash heap and flipped them back to the waiting infield: pills, nylon kit bags, a bird guide, pages well-chewed. Later, safely out of the bear's private zone, we took stock. He still had vitamin B, Benadryl and Zantac. Not bad, I thought. Bears are supposed to know all about medicinal plants. This modern bear figures chemistry can provide what he needs: bug repellant, an after-insect treatment, a good antacid in case he gets lucky in scrounging. I felt less annoyed and more interested in these encounters. What touching patience a wild animal showed in tolerating our nearness.

What name I called him made no difference at all to makwa, I'm sure, but it made a difference to me. "Bear" keeps me within the ways my own culture has taught me to see them, cuddly or ominous. *Karhu* is better, one of the few Finnish words I know, a word from my childhood that makes me think of my family's nervous kinship with those other blueberry pickers. But saying makwa brings me closer to my own somewhat shaky conviction that the animal and I may actually understand each other.

Legend says we all had a common language once, two-legged, four-legged and winged. Children often know this. Even before I could read, I fervently believed that vivid scene in *Through the Looking Glass*: Alice wandering in the wood of forgetfulness, her arm around the soft neck of a fawn. At the border, conventional wisdom returns and the fawn flees with the heartbreaking words, "Why, I'm a fawn, and you're a human child!" Another version of The Fall: Humans and animals violated the original covenant, and the Great Spirit scrambled our languages. Makwa is the four-legged who is believed still most tuned to human speech; he should not be spoken of rudely.

The time is sliding by so peacefully that I almost forget why I'm awake. The only moment of alarm comes when a breeze throws sparks at my Gore-Tex wind pants, which I shouldn't be wearing by a fire anyway. The only disruptive noises are our own. Pussyfooting around to fix coffee, I drop the pot lid with a resounding clank. Joan falls off her log, and we try to stifle our snorts of laughter. She goes to bed, replaced by sleepy Louise, who trips over a pair of boots and falls onto a tent.

"Hey!" growls a gruff voice, the one people use hoping to impress large disobedient dogs, or bears. Louise needs the coffee more — I hand her the mug. Organic Peruvian, fine-ground, nonbleached filters. On a dry, starry night. This is not exactly hardship duty.

Nor are the bears, come to think of it, a major problem. I've made it past irrational resentment, my sense of being put upon. The most we can claim is that they are making us give up the illusion that we control where we camp, how fast we eat, when we can sleep. The sleep deprivation is harder on our kayakers than our canoeists; rocked on the waves, one fell dead asleep in her boat. But she didn't actually fall out. And, so far, no bear has insisted we leave a site on a day when Lake Superior's winds make paddling dangerous or flat-out impossible.

The bears do take up a lot of time, but what else do we have to do? We came here to see wildlife and can hardly object when the sightings aren't on our terms. I'm getting acclimated to our visitors, and my concern has shifted: If the bears here become too acclimated, camp bears, it may mean there are too many travelers. I've thought I'd keep coming here until my hair is white. Now I wonder if I should, or want to, come back. Pukaskwa seems a little less wild.

I'm afraid the old compact between humans and wild bears — mutual respect and avoidance — is breaking down, and this generation of bears is involved in a game with us. Fortunately no one here is panicked, so when we play the game back — chasing the bear away, hiding food, covering our flanks — we're a smooth team. Most of the women are veterans of many long canoe trips, but even Louise, age sixty-five and on her first real wilderness trip, is unflappable, treating the bears like one of the four boisterous sons she raised. Instead of sleeping, here she is, cheerily watching by the fire, not wanting to miss anything. I think about how we learn fear, and think that these women don't displace onto bears their ordinary anxieties about life, nor invest bears with whatever primal terrors we all harbor or try to deny.

———————————⟋———————————

Four o'clock, four-forty. I glance idly at my watch now and then, and don't wake my replacement. I don't want to miss any of this night. Cassiopeia is winking at us, but already most stars are fading out. Ordinary day will come soon enough.

Thirty-eight years of canoe trips and this is the first time I've had a bear problem, if I want to call it that. And yet how often bears have been elusive companions, leaving cryptic messages of their parallel lives. On the bank of Hilda Creek, where we camped, those deep shadowy tracks with sand grains still crumbling into the claw marks, and the faint acrid smell of alarm. On the Rum Lake portage, a broad ribbon of stench that floated across our path like invisible smoke, vivid as the bear itself. On a solo trip, on the Stony River, the bear who appeared next to me as I napped, an oddly comforting presence. I'm not sure the bear had a physical form.

For such massive beings, bears have a remarkable ability to vanish like fog, like ghosts. They also seem to have an acute sense of the appropriate. My home river, the Vermilion, 1978: We met bear hunters who whined that while they were out putting down baits, a bear had raided their camp and stolen all their food. Turtle River, northern Ontario, 1980: Wide bear trails everywhere, but a bear appeared only to one woman, who was grieving, and wanted just one thing from the trip, to see a bear. Vermilion River, 1988: Sharon came hoping to overcome her fear of bears so she could go solo camping. A bear visited politely one rainy evening and returned as we slept, leave large, impressive piles of "sign" right behind a tent, and near the tarp where we slept, but never touching our food packs. Sharon said she was ready to camp alone.

Even these present bears, so chummy around our camps, have an aspect that's out past the edge of what I know. Early in the morning after the first raid, hoping to retrieve what might be left of our condiments, we went searching in the thick, mossy forest where he had most insistently hung around. Following my intuition and a faint track up the steep hill, I came out into a sunny clearing on a cliff overlooking the lake, and saw a flash of red. It was not our sack, but a small cloth banner, stirring in the breeze.

Below, on the gray bedrock and soft lichens, was a big circle of tiny cloth bundles, tobacco ties, I knew, a hundred or two hundred of them, yellow, white, red, black, the sacred colors. The circle enclosed two small, perfect clusters of birch and a bed of balsam boughs. Someone had been here seeking a vision. The cloth was faded but not decaying. This spring, I guessed; it would have been a dangerous trip coming alone by canoe, or a long hike down the coastal trail.

I kept a respectful distance. The moment I saw those bright tobacco bundles, my heart lifted. An old faith was still alive, and someone was acting out a deep relationship between humans and this place. It made time and life seem more spacious and deeper. The young leaves of the birches were silver-edged, distinct and hard. Far below, Lake Superior glittered in the sun, icy and dangerous, that beautiful water cold enough to kill me in minutes, should I capsize. I had never before been so acutely aware of danger, in every cell. At the same time I knew it was worth taking risks, paddling here, a place that had things to teach me. Something powerful seemed intact, and the bear was part of it.

Back down at the beach, I mentioned what I'd seen, but only briefly. I was glad no one else climbed up — it kept the privacy of the place. We located our shredded spice sack (powdered eggs and honey gone, of course, but garlic and tarragon vinegar remained), and as soon as we had it, the bear reappeared. I had the feeling he'd been watching us a long time. He watched us scramble to finish packing, and stood right on shore as we paddled away.

Five o'clock, full soft light. Definitely, it's time to catch a quick nap, but I bargain about bedtime, as I did in kindergarten. I'll sleep after the first bird call, I promise myself. Too soon, there's a hermit thrush, far away. But it's the winter wren who on this trip is around every day, our companion bird; I should wait for it. A few minutes later, a wren starts up his long, self-confident piccolo trills. So I wake Jesse to take my place, kick off my boots, and crawl into the sleeping bag. Five fifteen. As I drift off, there's a faint, familiar sound. Tap tap-atap tap tap. The bear box. I fall asleep.

"Hey! You! *Drop* that spray skirt!" Louise's hearty voice wakes me. I roll back out of the tent. Five twenty. Big trouble, I fret, if a kayak spray skirt is torn or gone. But the bear has taken only an optional canoe spray cover, and a paddle, leaving a funny, beavertail track down the sand. Louise trots back down the beach toward me, wearing a big grin.

"Wish I had a photo of that bear taking off with that spray cover flapping. It looked so *pleased* with itself. Like my dog playing keep-away."

The bear ambles back, empty-mouthed; he sits back and scratches his ears. While we watch, he takes a dump on the beach, a splendid gesture of disrespect or unconcern, if we choose to take it that way. Once more we organize into platoons to hold him at bay, to track down our gear, to manage the strategic retrieval of breakfast from the bear box. The teenage bear wanders off to see what he can stir up at the next site up the bay. As we pack up, I realize I'm already planning my next trip here.

———————⟡———————

Postscript: The park wardens closed these campsites for a few weeks. At the end of the summer, there had been no further bear incidents. Our youngsters had found another way to make a living.

AUTUMN

Time slows and the bird is in suspension and everything feels right. The gun comes up smoothly, the bird is the all. Everything is focused on the bird in the air, and you dismiss all else.

JOEL M. VANCE
From *Drummers*

An Old Dog Dreams

LARRY M. GAVIN

I know in your sleep
Old dog, you are not
An old dog,
But a creature outside of time
Propelled by scent through a dream
Unfolding like a flower in your
Sleeping brain.
Scent melding taste to image
Making all
An old dog needs to live
The memory of scent, I mean.
In these final years
You seem to take nourishment
From air-made images
Of pheasant, partridge, rabbit,
Grouse, and autumn.
Smell charged with some strange
Electricity as it signals
Sleeping legs to run
In unrested slumber on the couch.
You chase pheasants across
The endless prairie at sunset, don't you?
But now sunset made perfect.

You never fail to
Solve the riddle of aroma
Building to a powerful perfume at flush
Brilliant as sunlight on cattails
In November.
I like to hope my smell
Is there with you
I'd love to be timeless too
And stupid
As I was back then
Until you, old dog,
Taught me wisdom.
Wise to the ways of dogs
At least. The kind of
Wisdom that arrives like a good dream
From who knows where
Like fragrance, old age
And flight.

Published by permission of the author.
This poem first appeared in *Gun Dog* magazine.

Joel Vance has explored the Minnesota out-doors for many years, canoeing, hunting and fishing from the Boundary Waters to the Iowa line. He spent twen-ty-two years as an award-winning news and magazine writer for the Missouri Department of Conservation, then became a full-time freelance writer with three magazine columns and many articles to his cred-it. He has published four books and one book on tape and has another book due out in 1998. He has received the Excellence in Craft award from the 2,000-member Outdoor Writers Association of America and has won its top con-servation writing honor. He is also a past presi-dent, two-time board member and board chair-man of OWAA. His books include Brush, Bobs and Brittanies, Grandma and the Buck Deer, Confessions of an Outdoor Maladroit, *and a book on tape collection of short stories,* Billy Barnstorm, The Birch Lake Bomber.*

JOEL M. VANCE

Drummers

JOEL M. VANCE

" There probably still was snow on the ground, and the bog was tight with ice when the bird began to drum in earnest. Somehow it knew that winter had grown weak and life was stirring under the earth's chill skin. "

There is a log.

It is physically no different from a thousand other trees gone to earth, quietly fading into the muck of a Minnesota bog. Except that there is a pocketknife stuck into its skin, and in memory that knife glints in the golden October late afternoon sun, sticky with apple juice.

Perhaps I could find the log and retrieve the knife, but the knife would be rusty and perhaps the day overcast and sullen, and the memory would change from gold to gray. The knife is sharp and clean in memory, and the dog is with me. It was on this log that I sat and sliced a Jonathan apple and shared it with my Brittany and looked at the cock bird, the drummer, dead at my feet.

The bird was in a shaft of sunlight, filtering through the popple, limp in death, gray tail partly fanned. The tail was long, the longest I've ever claimed, as befitting the king of the covert. I believe this was his drumming log. Could be. It fit the formula. Bit of overhead cover, open arena in front, a stage on which the big bird would strut each spring, posturing for females, performing drumrolls as old as sound, a cutting contest with upstart rivals.

He owned this neck of the woods until I came along. Oh, sure, he risked death from above — the silent great horned owl falling on him like a shroud or the stiletto-like attack of a woodland hawk. But mostly the forest belonged to him. He was tougher than the other male grouse and quicker than any predatory sortie, up to, but not including, a charge of No. 7 1/2 lead shot.

He was a fully gray-tailed bird. Sometimes there are red-tailed grouse and sometimes a combination phase, but the general rule is that the farther north you go in ruffed grouse range, the more gray-tailed birds you find. Red-tailed birds aren't common where there still are a few timberwolves and the air smells of conifers.

This probably was a two-year-old bird, a senior citizen by grouse standards. It had been a long time and a world of peril since he tried to learn to drum, grabbing futilely at the air with his cupped wings. Then maybe he achieved a bit of sonic boom, then a better one, until finally he was percussing on his log like a veteran vaudevillian with a perfected act.

The cock bird found this old log when the sap began to rise in its body just as sap was rising in the winter-stark trees around it. Perhaps it had to wrest the log from another male; more likely it took possession of a log left vacant by another male that wasn't quick enough off the mark when a horned owl dropped by.

There probably still was snow on the ground, and the bog was tight with ice when the bird began to drum in earnest. Somehow it knew that winter had grown weak and life was stirring under the earth's chill skin. Grouse all over the woods came to their drumming logs and began thundering their eternal challenge.

I doubt any other hunter had visited this swamp corner — Minnesota is filled with places not seen by man since time began. It's easy to find them, harder to explore them. Northern Minnesota has many thousands of acres marked "State of Minnesota Tax Forfeited" on the plat maps. No signs say that someone's dream went bust there. It's taxpayer land, but you won't find any taxpayers stumbling through the rank popple, fighting a maze of bogholes on the thin promise of a grouse flush.

The grouse had gone through a couple of springs on this log, drumming by moonlight, staking out territory. Almost certainly a hen bird would have investigated this fine fellow. She would have slipped silently in, like someone late to the show. He'd have seen her and paused in his drumming. Then the Elizabethan ruff of neck feathers that gives him his name would have expanded, forming a blue-black collar.

His tail fan would have expanded into full extension with an audible "snap!" and he would have paraded back and forth on the log, hissing and swaying, declaring his lust as ardently as a bawdy sonnet. At that moment, he was as vulnerable as he'd ever be, but no fox or bobcat was watching, and he got away with passion's temporary insanity.

Grouse drum year-round. I heard one last grouse season, drumming impudently as five of us worked through a covert. The drummer was at the edge of the covert, facing a pasture, but he must have known we were there. The dogs' locator collars beeped, and Salty's German silver bell tinkled like that of a Salvation Army volunteer at Christmas.

There was the occasional virulent outburst of Anglo-Saxon instruction to the dogs, who always think they know more about grouse hunting than humans do and who almost invariably are correct. You'd think, with all that danger about, a grouse would keep his wings shut.

But that drummer either was incredibly arrogant or incredibly stupid. Grouse lack arrogance, so it must have been a dumb drummer. Not so dumb, though, that when Spence Turner tried a sneak, he didn't flush into the brush and escape.

"He's been there all season," Ted said. Ted hunts the coverts until weather forces him out, and he appreciates survivor grouse. I think he was pleased that the drummer survived another threat. We left the bird to his log and his music.

The drummer I shot had played out his string. There were a wealth of outcomes where he lived; only one where he died. He could have crouched as we passed unknowing on the other side of the finger of woods. He could have run and flushed silently and never been detected. He could have flushed with a fluster and verve that caused me to miss.

But he didn't. He was in the path of the dog and the dog pointed and the bird flushed straightaway and I shot him. Death feeds on life. The grouse would loll on a bed of wild rice, and we'd exclaim over his tender succulence, but whatever is the essence of grouse will stay in the woods until next spring when a new drummer takes over.

Nature is impatient. There's always something jittering in the background, waiting for something to get out of the way. Including us. Including the Brittany drowsing at my feet. He'd grown old in the grouse woods. We both had together, come to think of it. Being a dog, he aged quicker than I did. Only his keen passion for hunting remained untouched by time. Like me, he would hunt until he dropped, wake stiff in the morning, and do it again.

I didn't know then that this would be the last grouse we would share, the last sunlit break and the last tart Jonathan. He was the drummer of the kennel, the elder statesdog. A thousand hunts, a thousand birds lay behind. He had bounced through the woods, just as he always did, with the eager joy of hunting. I wonder if his savage lupine ancestors took such great pleasure in the act of hunting. Wolves live or die based on how well they hunt. Maybe that takes the fun out of it. Guff and I would go home to a nice dinner whether we killed a grouse or not.

Guff went on point at the base of the finger of woods, near the old log. Chances are, the drummer never strayed more than a hundred yards from the log. It was the center of his existence, once he claimed it and defended it. The grouse seemed checked in midair, the way it sometimes happens. Time slows and the bird is in suspension and everything feels right. The gun comes up smoothly, the bird is the all. Focus—everything is focused on the bird in the air, and you dismiss all else.

The bird fluffed and folded at the shot, and I knew it was dead in the air. No need to worry about a runner. I walked forward and got the bird from Guff and then we sat on the log and I peeled the apple and stuck my knife in the log.

The grouse is gone and so is the dog. They live only in my memory, and when I am gone, there will be no memory at all of that afternoon in the sunlight. The drumming log still is there and will be for years until it collapses into humus and the knife stuck in it becomes a rusted, unidentifiable lump.

But for now this old drummer looks toward tomorrow and remembers yesterday, and the knife is sharp and bright and the dog drowses and waits to go on into the day.

JOHN WEISS

John Weiss was born in Brainerd, where he learned to fish with his father, Wilfred, and Wayne Jenkins on North Long Lake, or fished by himself on Gilbert Lake. He also loved to walk the lowlands along the Mississippi, "but I never learned to hunt until I married Debbie, whose father and brothers were avid duck hunters." They introduced him to The Point, a hunting ground that provides the setting for the accompanying story. John is now outdoor and environmental editor and photographer for the Rochester Post-Bulletin. *In southeast Minnesota, he has learned to love the blufflands and the Mississippi backwaters, where he continues to fish, hunt, canoe and camp. He lives in Rochester with Debbie and children Angela and Charlie. His oldest son, John, is in college.*

The Last Star in Orion's Belt

JOHN WEISS

"To the east, we see a fiery sunrise, the sun burning the bellies of gray clouds light red, then blaze orange. I take little notice, having seen it before, but Charlie loves it and implores me to look again. The spectacular hues remind me that sometimes the teacher can learn from the student. "

In the darkness outside, the wind ripples the tips of the aspens. It will be another windy morning hunting ducks on The Point.

We have already endured one morning of soaking rain and north wind, another of a bombastic west wind that kept us from our favorite blinds, and one with a southeast wind that tossed our decoys wildly. This will be our last morning, and we hope for calm, so that we can watch the three stars in Orion's belt reflected in Birch Lake and feel the anxiety and hope when only Alnilak, the star on the left, remains, and it is shooting time. Maybe, just maybe, we will see the big flocks of bluebills again come into the lake.

But that is some hours away. I go back to sleep as the wind continues to pound the aspens. At 5:45, the alarm goes off, and the ritual begins. Chuck Hubbard, patriarch, slips on his heavy clothes, like those he has worn for more than forty years of hunting bluebills, canvasbacks, mallards and ringnecks on The Point in the mid-Minnesota lake. His gun, the Winchester Model 12 he has shot for most of those years, leans against the wall, scratched and worn, but dependable. He cases the gun and heads out, putting on his beaten cowboy hat with the Marine Corps emblem on the front.

Tom Hubbard, his son, readies himself, too. He's been watching or taking part in these hunts since he was three and now drives six hours round trip each weekend during duck season, at least whenever the lake is open.

I entered this tradition when I married Chuck's daughter more than two decades ago. I wasn't a duck hunter then. Chuck gave me my first shotgun, making me find it by following clues to its hiding place in an old outhouse near the cabin. With fifteen years at The Point, I am a budding veteran who came in at the end of the peak times, when the big bluebill flocks poured in and waited their turn to land among the decoys.

Charlie, my son, quickly puts on his clothes. They're hand-me-downs and some of my extras, but he doesn't care — he's going to The Point with his grandpa. And this year, he has that mint-condition Winchester Model 12 Chuck gave him three days ago. At age thirteen, he's well versed in the morning ritual but has much to learn about hunting. It's my turn to teach him, as Chuck and Tom taught me.

The ritual is precise. We know how long it will take to dress, drive to Chuck's land, open the gate, go down the road, load the boats and set out decoys. We time each segment to the second, give or take ten minutes for a balky outboard or whitecap wind. In fifteen minutes, we are dressed, the cabin lights are out, and we've piled into the truck. Driving the four miles to the landing, we listen to the radio, impatient for the end of "Moon River" and the beginning of the weather. Finally, the announcer declares southeast winds, four miles per hour. Bending treetops and grasses tell us his direction might be right, but he's dead wrong on speed. It will be hard putting out decoys and even harder taking them in.

The road for the last mile is guarded by a gate, "with character," as Chuck would say. It has a deep bow on the top of one side where a quaking aspen fell and smacked it; the bottom scrapes the ground. We give no thought to fixing it. Charlie runs out, unlocks the gate, and we drive through. He locks it again and is back in forty-four seconds. The kid's good. We're training him to break thirty-eight.

The road is rutted and grassy, but open. Clearing toppled aspens and brush before the hunting opener is another of our rituals. At the small parking area, we grab our gear and head down the catwalk, an ancient structure of planking of old outhouse walls. As we cross, brush jumps out of the dark and whacks our faces. Like the gate, the catwalk has character, though we don't appreciate it when the boards are frosted with sleet.

We find we were right about the wind — rough and southeast. Bad for ducks. Northwest winds are better; their cold gusts bring in ducks that swing wide and come in from the south, where we can see them. On a southeast wind, ducks sneak in from behind. Charlie listens as we discuss who will hunt where, and why.

The four of us and Tom's dog, Jake, squeeze into a fishing boat, along with shotguns and other gear. We tie on an aluminum double-pointer with four bags of duck decoys and several large goose decoys. Tom cranks up the old Johnson three-horse motor that takes more than ten minutes to push us less than a mile — it beats rowing. Venus is bright in the east, but clouds moving in from the west are covering Orion. When the stars are out, we know we only have to watch that constellation. When Alnalam and Mintaka fade, and only Alnilak glimmers, it's a half-hour before sunrise and time to shoot.

Through the darkness, as we motor slowly west, we can make out trees on a low spit of land that elbows into the lake. The Point. Chuck and Tom go around to the calm west, while Charlie and I take the tip. I row the double-pointer and Charlie puts out the battered decoys that have bobbed and danced on the waves for years. Many have their own names, like Olga and Sven. Chuck likes to give names to things — all loons are Elmer, all beavers are Joe.

Setting our decoys in the wind is frustrating business, but we eventually get out two pods with a gap where we hope the divers will land. Then we go back to the blind and settle in to wait, hoping the clouds will clear Orion. We are dressed warm, but a shot of hot chocolate helps. Charlie and I sit close together, like hundreds of other hunters who have waited here before, seeing the same constellation, hoping for the big flocks, waiting for memories to be made.

Three days earlier, before Tom arrived, Chuck sat behind the blind and watched as Charlie and I hunted. He is past seventy; shooting birds doesn't mean much to him now. He started hunting The Point in 1954, while working at a small machine company, of which he would become part owner and later president. The company co-leased The Point one year, and the hunters loved it because of the bluebills. "Oodles, thousands of them," Chuck says. "The sky was just covered with them. It was easy to get a limit of ten in two hours."

The lake was different then, too — more cattails and wild rice, shallower water, more hunters to move the ducks around. Fewer waterfowlers visit the lake now, but the Patriarch has stayed. He bought The Point and the land around it when he retired. There are too may memories there for him not to keep hunting. He remembers the time bluebills were stacked up by the thousands in a little bit of open water. He used a wooden boat to get there, ruining the boat, but getting some great shooting. Bluebills, a tasty diver duck, were once The Point's main attraction. Today, it's a smattering of this and that, often ringnecks that move in smaller flocks and don't decoy as well. Bluebills seem to have moved their migration west.

"They are fickle, fickle ducks," Chuck says.

Once Chuck starts telling Charlie about the old days, the stories roll. He tells how he and his other son, Chuckie, once emptied their shotguns at a flock of bluebills and missed, but as they sat down, five ducks hit the water — members of another flock flying behind.

Or the time Chuck's gun froze as he was rowing out to pick up a crippled bird but suddenly went off, blowing a hole in the side of the boat. Or the exploits of Sam, a four-year-old yellow Lab who would sit in front of the blind and not move when the hunters fired. On command, he would swim out and pick up ducks. Or the time when the lake was nearly frozen, but Chuck and his sons managed to make it to The Point.

"It was a great big flock, and they kept coming. They were just hanging in the air in front of us." They dropped nine birds with nine shells. "I've hunted in some cold weather," Chuck says. "You haven't lived until you've hunted bluebills on ice."

Charlie listens, taking it all in. "It must have been great," he says. "I can only dream of that."

Chuck's company once built a small hunting shack behind The Point, with bunks, heat and a kitchen. Chuck would carry his children down the catwalk to the boat and take them to the shack for the weekend. In the morning, while the hunters shot ducks, his wife, Angie, cooked breakfast. Eventually, Chuck bought land on a nearby lake and built a summer cabin. After that, the hunting shack fell into disuse.

Through the years, Chuck has hunted with his wife, children, daughter-in-law, son-in-law, grandchildren, friends, business partners, his children's friends, sister and brother-in-law, and some people he can't remember inviting. Each left the landing in the dark and saw The Point emerge silhouetted against the western sky. Each added to the lore of the hunt.

Our four-day hunt will go down as the Weekend of the Horrible Winds. Chuck could not remember such ugly gales churning the lake. One morning, the motor conked out, and we tried to row to The Point. After nearly an hour, we still hadn't made it. We settled for a slightly calm area near the old hunting shack. After a fruitless hour, we picked up the decoys. Charlie was hungry for the steak and eggs breakfast at the Spotlite Cafe in Garrison.

On the final day of the weekend, we make it to The Point. To the east, we see a fiery sunrise, the sun burning the bellies of gray clouds light red, then blaze orange, a rendition of a Martian sky. I take little notice, having seen it before, but Charlie loves it and implores me to look again. The spectacular hues remind me that sometimes the teacher can learn from the student. Still, the beauty of the sunrise does not compensate for the absence of ducks.

As shooting becomes legal, I again have rich hope for the day. Charlie and I had shot a few ducks in the previous three days, including a gadwall that decoyed beautifully. We both shot at the same instant, and the duck dropped to the water. Charlie claimed it — the first duck he shot with his Model 12. Since then, the shooting has been weak, but maybe today Charlie will see fifty or (dare I dream?) a hundred bluebills swing around twice and finally barrel in.

To tempt the ducks to come in, I teach Charlie some tricks. Like pouring coffee or hot chocolate. "Ducks love chocolate," I tell him. "They know when you're preoccupied and love to buzz in when you're not ready." Another trick is to stand up in the blind for a seventh-inning stretch. Or, best of all, to case your gun. That's guaranteed to attract every duck for miles.

The wind today again makes it impossible to hear ducks. It's wonderful to sit on a still morning and hear the sizzle and whistling of wings. On perfectly calm mornings, I've heard ducks sound as if they were ready to drop their wings and plow into the decoys. I'd grip my shotgun and slowly look, but see only specks, hundreds of yards overhead. In the wind, though, our ears are of little use. Still, it is warmer than if a northwest wind were pounding us. On those days, we've had waves roll over decoys and coat them thick with ice. But at least in a northwest wind, the ducks will fly. Given a choice between comfort and ducks, we'll take ducks.

Suddenly, five bluebills buzz us, swing, and come in hard from the northwest. That makes the morning worth fighting the wind. But hitting ducks landing into the wind is miserably tough shooting, the birds dipping and tossing like winged leaves. Charlie and I miss all five. Another flock comes by, and I take out one, a drake bluebill with a gray-checkered back. It's not a big northern bird, at least not as big as some I've seen.

As the morning wears on, clouds cover the sky, the wind streaks the lake with foam, and whitecaps tip some waves. Another half-hour of duckless skies and we case the guns. I cast a surreptitious glance at the sky, expecting a big flock to come in, but the old trick hasn't worked today. I row the double-pointer while Charlie scoops up foam canvasback decoys, hollow plastic bluebills, and fat Olga. He's getting the hang of handling decoys in rough weather, of snagging them as the boat tips and bobs. It takes hard rowing just to keep the boat in place and all my strength to move it against the wind. If I take two breaths without rowing, we lose twenty feet.

Chuck and Tom join us. Tom has shot one hooded merganser. We all get into the fishing boat and take off, dragging the double-pointer. I turn back and see The Point getting slowly smaller as the little three-horse fights the waves. We unload, but on a lark check a nearby pothole for ducks. We're in luck — three mallards are feeding on the calm side. Charlie takes his place between Tom and me, knowing he's part of the hunting party, no longer an outsider.

We drop all three ducks. They will make an excellent dish, the one we know as Grandpa Duck's recipe, a concoction with white wine, served over rice. Only ducks we've shot are good enough for that hallowed meal.

As we leave Chuck's land, Charlie hops out, opens the gate, waves us through with a flourish, locks the gate, and is back inside the truck in 42.8 seconds. The kid's getting better.

Shawn Perich is an outdoor writer from Hovland, Minn., a small community on the North Shore of Lake Superior, near the Canadian border.

SHAWN
PERICH

A native of the Northwoods, he is a lifelong grouse hunter who fishes for steelhead and brook trout during the "off season." He shares his home with his companion, Vikki, and their two dogs: Casey, a yellow Lab; and Abby, a German shepherd.

Fool Hens

SHAWN PERICH

> **North country grouse fly only if they must. In a dense forest, it is easier to run than fly. In autumn, a grouse could flush straight into the talons of a migrating hawk. A safe grouse is one that is on the ground in heavy cover, sheltered from flying predators by a canopy of balsam and spruce.**

During September and October, drive-by shootings are commonplace in northern Minnesota. A pickup truck slides to a halt on the gravel road, the gunman steps out and bang! — another pebble-picking partridge is flapping in the dust. Here in the Northwoods, such assassinations are called grouse hunting.

Now, before you slam this book shut in disgust, consider this: rare is the Northwoods pot-shooter who goes anywhere he can't drive a pickup truck or an all-terrain buggy. That leaves most of the birds and millions of public acres for hunters who like to walk. But here's the catch: the challenge lies not in finding grouse but in flushing them.

Meet the fool hen. Although these unsophisticated bumpkins were eliminated from the ruffed grouse gene pool in more populated regions a century ago, they still flourish in northern Minnesota's vast forests. Run low on ammo and you can kill them with rocks. (A friend of mine beaned a snow goose and blue goose last fall, but that's another story.) If they do flush, often they'll fly no farther than the nearest balsam. So why hunt these suicidal tree chickens? Well, for every fool hen, there's another grouse out there that will make a fool out of you.

A few years ago I went hunting with Sam Cook, a writer from Duluth, in the rugged hills on the Grand Portage Indian Reservation, a wild hunk of real estate wedged between Lake Superior's North Shore and the Canadian border. The first grouse flushed by my late yellow Lab, Rebel, fluttered up about twenty feet and landed in a balsam. Now, your average jack pine savage would have levelled a bead on the fool hen's head and sent it to the great aspen thicket in the sky, but Sam is from Kansas. In Kansas when you flush a bird, it flies away. Sam, a consummate sportsman, went over to kick and shake the balsam so I could shoot the bird when it flew. At first the grouse was unperturbed. When Sam's kung fu efforts became annoyingly vigorous, the bird finally flushed from the far side of the tree and neither of us got a shot. Fool hen indeed.

Actually, it's unfair to call northern grouse fool hens. Instead, look at this scene from the bird's point of view. Rebel's approach was no different from that of a fox or timber wolf, both of which a grouse can easily avoid by flying into the nearest evergreen. Sam's kicks and shakes were little threat, because he wasn't climbing the tree like a pine marten. The grouse saw me and flushed from the other side of the tree so, just in case I was a giant goshawk, I couldn't give pursuit.

North country grouse fly only if they must. "I feel that, with few exceptions, a grouse in flight is a grouse in trouble," wrote the late Gordon Gullion in his 1984 classic, *Grouse of the North Shore*. "The hazards of flight, including predation and accidental death, usually outweigh the advantages."

Again we need to think like a partridge. In a dense forest, it is easier to run than fly. And in autumn, a grouse could flush straight into the talons of a migrating hawk. A safe grouse is one that is on the ground in heavy cover, sheltered from flying predators by a canopy of balsam and spruce. Start thinking like a bird, and suddenly that foolish behavior seems pretty smart.

Thus educated to the ways of fool hens, you are better prepared to hunt them. Exasperation is just part of the game. Even if you convince a bird to flush, it may barrel off unseen into some of the thickest tangles you'll find this side of the tropics. Rare indeed is the grouse that flushes into the open, except during deer season. The only time I ever flushed a covey of grouse in an open meadow was when I was carrying a 30.06. However, last year I finally flushed a bird in a forty-acre clear-cut — twice. I fired four shots without touching a feather. Fooled again.

Maybe the shot was too easy. I'm more accustomed to shooting at feathered rockets whizzing through brief openings in the balsams. Sometimes, you don't even know if you made the shot until the dog comes back with the bird. A few years ago, Rebel put up a late-season bird inside a conifer thicket. The bird was fifty yards out when it came into view. However, I was using the same loads that I'd used to kill Iowa roosters at similar ranges the week before. I fired as the grouse was about to disappear into the cover. For a long time, Rebel crashed through the tangles and blowdowns in the direction the bird had gone. *You're nuts, dog*, I thought. *That bird was home free*. Then he came back with the bird.

You learn to trust the dog in this game. Although I've shot dozens of grouse while hunting without one, the dogless hunter doubtless walks by many birds that either sit tight or sneak away. Grouse will hold as tight as any rooster pheasant. Last November, while pussy-footing through the woods in search of venison, I happened upon a grouse holding court beneath a fallen tree. Softly and slowly, just a couple of steps at a time, I approached within fifteen feet. The partridge ducked its head and silently slipped beneath the tree. Although I passed within ten feet of the bird's hiding place, it remained hidden.

Now, I know how Rebel would have handled that bird. Zigzagging through the brush until he hit the scent, he'd then pour on the coal and roar down on the bird like a runaway locomotive. The grouse would have no choice but to flush. If it decided to land in a nearby balsam, Reb would try to climb the tree. If that failed to dislodge the grouse, he'd stand beneath the tree and bark until I arrived. There was no need for a bell or a beeper with that dog.

A grouse in a tree presents some special problems. If a barking dog can't convince a grouse to flush, how will you change its mind? Kicking the tree is only marginally effective (and rather Kansas of you). If the bird does flush, most likely you'll be off balance and unable to shoot. Instead, try throwing sticks or stones. Still, it may take a few tries, or a direct hit, to send the grouse airborne. Then you'll have a second or two to swing and fire before the bird disappears into the cover. Obviously, this isn't high-percentage shooting.

The best time to find fool hens holding in cover where they'll fly off when flushed is during the short window between the October leaf drop and the onset of winter. Where I hunt near the Canadian border, that window may last a few days or a few weeks. October snowstorms are not unusual. Even if it doesn't snow, many late autumn days are rendered unhuntable by raw, northwest winds. Grouse are tough to find on windy days, even in boom years when the birds are at the peak of their population cycle. And anyone who has ever watched an impetuous gust snap the crown off a fifty-foot aspen knows there are safer times to go hunting.

The hunting is best on drab, still days when the sky and the forest are the color of dirty dishwater. The leaf-looking tourists have gone home and even the road-hunters have thinned out. The moose rut is winding down, so you're less likely to meet a belligerent bull in a clear-cut. If the nights haven't been cold enough yet to skim the beaver ponds, you may jump a few blacks or mallards. Best of all, you can see the grouse when they flush in the leafless woods.

I like to hunt along overgrown logging trails where the aspens are as thick as your wrist. Toss in some alder swamps, a few thick stands of spruce and balsam, and enough openings to grow clover, blueberries and wild rose, and you've got textbook grouse habitat. Although a month ago grouse could dine on anything from berries to mushrooms, hard frosts have frozen most of the items on that September menu. Clover is now the blue plate special, and it grows profusely between the ruts of forgotten logging roads.

A few years ago, I hiked a mile-long skid trail through an aspen thicket just north of the border in Ontario. Canadians hunt grouse much the same as Minnesotans do, except that even fewer of them walk up their birds. Grouse season had been open for a month, but Reb and I were almost certainly the first ones to walk that old logging road. Thinking the trail might lead to a beaver pond, I grabbed a handful of duck loads (you can use lead for waterfowl in Ontario) and a few grouse loads.

Sometimes everything goes right. The day was sunny and warm enough to be comfortable with just a wool shirt. The popples had just dropped their leaves, which covered the ground like yellow coins. The road was a swath of knee-high grass that sloped into a cut-over valley, with just enough wet spots to make you wish you had worn rubber boots. Rebel started working the thickets and soon flushed a woodcock that somehow dodged two well-placed shots. Then he flushed a grouse that wasn't so lucky. The leafless aspens offered no security for perching partridges, so the grouse flushed and flew. By the time we reached the overgrown log landing at the end of the road, I was two grouse shy of a five-bird limit and into the duck loads. I killed one more and scared another on the walk back to the pickup.

Another spur trail led off from where the truck was parked. I unloaded the birds from my game bag, grabbed some more shells, and started up the spur for grouse number five. The trail led into a dense thicket of young balsam and aspens as thick as my thigh. Apparently, the partridge were holding a convention there. Within a hundred yards, Rebel put up thirteen birds, most of which fluttered up into the impenetrable balsams or thundered away unseen. Number thirteen was the unlucky one that flew into the open and wound up in my game pouch.

Bonanzas such as this are always possible when you hunt in country where fool hens far outnumber the fools who pursue them. In a world of strip malls, subdivisions and posted property, elbow room like you find in the North is a scarce commodity. Few wing-shooters know the freedom of hunting forests so vast you can get lost in them, but my neighbor does. Every fall he tells me about the places where he's been partridge hunting. I think his goal is to see how far he can get from the nearest road. He likes to climb high ridges where you find sweeping views of Lake Superior or the inland canoe country. I've been to a few of those places myself. They're not the best places to look for birds, but the scenery makes up for it.

My neighbor grew up hunting farm country ducks and pheasants. He laughs about our fool hens, but their lack of sophistication certainly doesn't dampen his enthusiasm for hunting them. I suspect he is motivated less by weight in his game bag than by a restless urge to see new country. I know the feeling, and so does every trout fisherman who wonders what lies beyond the next bend in the stream.

The search for grouse or trout is just an excuse to keep going. What are we after? I'm not sure, but I'll always pause to investigate a pile of wolf scat to see what old *Canis lupus* had for dinner, or make a detour so I can grope through the tangled tag alders in a woodcock motel. One birdless day last fall, the only thing I carried from the woods was a weathered moose antler.

But grouse remain the object of these excursions; otherwise I'd have just as much fun leading girl scouts on nature hikes. So what if you must toss sticks at some birds to make them flush? Nobody's perfect. And if I'm a fool to hunt fool hens, then at least I'm a happy one.

Mike Strandlund is one of those many "boomerangers" who grew up in Minnesota, took off to find his fortune elsewhere, and realized it was here all

MIKE
STRANDLUND

along. As editor of Bowhunting World magazine, published in Minnetonka, he has the best of both worlds: an eighty-acre farm in western Hennepin County (the setting for the accompanying story) and a job that takes him on bowhunting adventures throughout the continent. He enjoys fishing, skiing, canoeing, dog training, horseback riding, and generally living the Minnesota lifestyle with children Bradley and Sara.

A Matter of Trust

MIKE STRANDLUND

" When I knew I had entered the deadly twenty-yard zone, I plucked an arrow from my bow quiver, sidled up to a bush, and raised slowly into shooting position. As I did, the doe's head snapped erect. We stood like two statues, each waiting for the other to make a move. "

It was several summers ago that I bought a farm in the hunting country of Minnesota. The secluded old homestead was at the end of a half-mile driveway and surrounded by fields home to pheasants, geese and deer. It was a place for solitude and independence, with eighty acres of elbow room for teaching kids and dogs how to hunt. The buildings were turn-of-the-century and we had to renovate our way into the house, but the pastoral life was well worth the work.

The idea was to have a big place to play and get gradually into as much farming as I cared to do. I'd start by renting out the cropland and feeding some cattle and hogs. Most folks figured we'd be raising our own meat, but not so. Our livestock would go to market to help make the tractor payments. My family had grown accustomed to eating meat harvested by my bow, and I wanted it to stay that way.

That grew on my mind as the overwhelming work of getting started began to subside and hunting season approached. I'd spotted a few deer in the hayfield beyond the barn, a ten-acre patch flanked by sharecrop corn. The deer had me pegged, too, but after a few panicked encounters, they seemed to get used to me. They kept their distance, nervously tolerating the new activity. I was enamored of the idea of hunting my own deer on my own farm. I could bowhunt free of long road trips and kissing up for permission. I could harvest some venison and reduce crop depredation, the proverbial brace of birds with a single stone. I started to lay out a plan.

A few does and their fawns were bedding in the high corn, coming out to graze on the succulent clover of the cutover field each dusk. As fall approached, a small buck occasionally appeared, always seeming to keep his distance from the does. I would save him for another year, or maybe for one of the neighbor kids who would really get excited over that small rack. I would target the big doe, the one with the fawn plenty old enough to make it on its own.

I had noticed the deer would enter my field from any of three sides, usually picking their approach to head into the wind. Their unpredictable routes, coupled with the lack of places to hang a tree stand, made stand hunting impractical. That was fine with me. I had been looking for a good situation to try my hand at stalking whitetails.

I regretfully missed out on the early part of the season. I had been hunting Colorado buglers in late September, and the fact that my freezer was not brimming with elk meat as planned made me even more interested in that venison store just out my back door. My opportunity came on a brisk October evening, the kind that makes aspen leaves rattle and prompts you to take mental stock of your firewood supply. I had been getting ready for a hunting trip up north with friends when I paused at an upstairs window to gaze toward the field, as had become a habit, and noticed a lone doe munching wilted clover. I glanced at my watch, grabbed my bow and camo coat, and hit the door.

I had to chuckle as I thought out my approach, a far cry from a classic stalk. Behind the old cookhouse and garage, through the derelict dairy barn, along the fenceline and up to the old silo, which I would peek around for a status report. Once there, I saw the deer remained in the clover, grazing heartily, about a hundred yards away. I tested the wind, then hunkered over and scampered a ways through the overgrown pasture grass. As I closed the gap I went into a crawl. The dry weeds were noisy, but I knew if I was careful to keep the racket to a minimum, the gusty breeze would cover for me.

At the fenceline rock pile I stopped to get my bearings again. I eased my eyes up to the level of the wavering weed tops and spotted the deer, closer than I expected, about thirty yards. I sank back down and weighed the pros and cons of either trying a shot from there or trying to sneak closer. Finally, I crawled on, carefully moving aside each crisp leaf and brittle stem in my path.

When I knew I had entered the deadly twenty-yard zone, I plucked an arrow from my bow quiver, sidled up to a bush, and raised slowly into shooting position. The deer was still there, still so intent on laying on its winter fat that I felt I could stand undetected for a perfect shot. As I did, the doe's head snapped erect. We stood, like two statues, each waiting for the other to make a move. My eyes instinctively began to focus on the doe's elbow as fingers strained eagerly on the bowstring. Then, uncannily, the deer buried her face back into the clover.

At the snap, the deer's head yanked up again. But she didn't run. She munched. She didn't even seem frightened by the sound — the sound of my arrow snapping back into its quiver. The doe blinked at me with a clump of clover hanging from both sides of her mouth, as if to say, "You've been acting strangely all summer. *Now* what are you up to?"

For some reason, I could not bring myself to send a sharp-tipped shaft into that peaceful scene. I realized then that this was an animal altogether different from any other game I had encountered. It did not view me as certain death on two legs. It knew me as the farmer she graciously shared her home with. This wasn't a matter of hunter and hunted, of a full or empty freezer, or even of life and death. It was a matter of trust.

In the farmhouse doorway, I paused to look back at the darkening field. The doe was still working over my hay. I noticed she'd been joined by her fawn, now nearly grown, but still scampering circles around her. I turned and went inside to finish packing for the morning hunt.

Gretchen Legler is an assistant professor in the Department of Creative Writing and Literary Arts at the University of Alaska-Anchorage, where she also co-directs the Program in Women's Studies. Her first book of nonfiction essays,

GRETCHEN LEGLER

All The Powerful Invisible Things: A Sportswoman's Notebook, *was published in 1995 by Seal Press. She is the recent recipient of a National Science Foundation Office of Polar Programs Artists and Writers grant, which took her to Antarctica for six months in 1997. She plans to create a collection of nonfiction essays from that experience. Her creative nonfiction and her short stories have appeared in* Uncommon Waters: Women Write About Fishing, A Different Angle: Flyfishing Stories by Women, *other anthologies and literary magazines. Her scholarship and reviews on literature and the environment have appeared in various journals and in several anthologies.*

Gooseberry Marsh

GRETCHEN LEGLER

> **Perhaps it was our own power we were eating. Perhaps it was our own ability to grow, to shoot, to find food for ourselves, that we were eating; our ability to engage creatively with the world. We were eating what we wanted so much. We were eating life.**

At Gooseberry Marsh, our canoe splits through thin ice. Craig and I push the silver bow against the frozen bank, and I gather up our ducks: ducks whose bodies I scooped from the water after they had fallen from the autumn sky, whose necks I had wrung one by one, whose blood is on my hands.

On shore, I slit their bellies with my pocketknife and reach two fingers into the sticky, velvet, still-hot caves, pulling out livers, lungs, the long cords the ducks speak through, and the hearts.

Gooseberry Marsh is a made-up name, pulled out of the air because the words felt full on our tongues. Swamp grass rings it. Goose nests on man-made pillars ring it. Sky rings it.

This year is a dry year, and going out at dawn, we had to pull our canoe over the shallow places between the two big ponds. The murky gas of rotting and growing things rose up from the craters our boots made in the mud. The mud, as deep as I am, wanted to pull me down, like hands to a bed.

After I have gutted them, I gather up our ducks in two hands and take them up the hill to the car. They swing by their soft orange feet against my thighs. Their bodies are still heavy. I line them up on the grass: three mallards, one small green teal, four bluebills, their beaks pointing toward the cattails where we hid, waiting for them to cup their wings and sail down into our decoys. I close each of their tiny eyes. In front of each mouth I dribble a minuscule amount of cornmeal from a box with a blue Quaker smiling. And then I grab handfuls of cornmeal and throw them — to the east, to the west, to the north, to the south, and where I am right now, the place I am standing with dead ducks at my feet.

What should be said?

I don't speak, but each time the grains of cornmeal fly out and hang for a moment in the air, then fall, I think of how we will eat these ducks — roast them quickly in a hot oven with only pepper and salt on the breasts, or roast them for hours in a big pan with raisins and apples. I think of how they will taste, how the kitchen will smell, and how, when we eat, someone will roll one of the pellets that killed these birds around and around on their tongue.

Snow starts to fall on the marsh, the flakes taken up into the pond, dissolving like wafers. The sky is the color of steel. I have saved their eight hearts. When Craig comes up from the canoe with the last load — a camouflage tarp and a bag of decoys — I give him half of the hearts and we walk down to the water, the hearts small and soft in our palms, like beads of dough, and we throw them back to the sky, calling out loud, fly!

Before the hearts fall into the amber water, I see wings unfold and mallards and teal and bluebills rising up.

Part of what hunting meant to us, when we were together, was feasting. It wasn't the shooting that mattered, but what we did with this food we gathered: how we prepared the ducks to eat, how we shared them with friends, how we raised our glasses before we ate, at a long table lit by candles, covered with a lacy white cloth, and thanked the ducks for their lives. Several times a year, at Easter, at Thanksgiving and at Christmas, Craig and I prepared banquets for our friends. Nearly everything we cooked for our feasts was from our garden, or collected from the woods, or killed by us. This, I think now, was why I hunted and still want to. Because I want this kind of intimate relationship with the food I eat.

There were some things — flour, sugar, oranges, walnuts and chutney — that Craig and I served at our feasts that we could not grow or collect ourselves. And for these items I would shop at our local grocery store. To get to the checkout counter in the store, I usually walked down the meat aisle. There was hardly ever a whole animal for sale, only parts. There were double-breasted cut-up fryers with giblets. Three-legged fryers and budget packs — two split breasts, two wings, two legs, two giblets and two necks. There were boneless, skinless thighs; packages of only drumsticks; plastic containers of livers. There were breaded, skinless, boneless breasts in a thin box — microwaveable, ninety-five percent fat-free, shrink-wrapped, "all natural" and farm fresh.

The meat cases were cool, so cool I could hardly smell the meat, only a sanitary wateriness. The smell was different from the smell of wet ducks and blood in the bottom of our canoe. The smell was different from the smell of the warm gut-filled cavity I reached my hand into when I cleaned the bird. The smell was different from the smell in the kitchen when we pulled out all the ducks' feathers, piling them up in a soft mound on the kitchen table; different from the smell when we dipped the birds in warm wax, wax that we then let harden and pulled off in thick flakes along with the ducks' pinfeathers.

The birds in the store were pared down and down so that what was left had no relationship to what these animals were when they were alive. They were birds cut and sliced until all that remained were grotesque combinations of named parts. It always felt obscene to me. What were those birds like whole? It was hard, standing amid the dry coolness rising up from the meat cases, to imagine any life; hard to construct a picture of these birds flying, walking, making morning noises, pecking for insects in the grass, fighting over corn, laying eggs. Hard to imagine them in any way but stacked in their airless cages.

One year, two weeks before Christmas, Craig and I invited twelve of our friends to our house for a feast. We spent all day preparing for this meal. I sliced through the dense brilliant layers of three red cabbages and set the purple shreds to simmer in a pot with honey. I stuffed our ducks with apples and oranges and onions and raisins, and spread the slippery pale breasts with butter and garlic, sprinkling on thyme and rosemary. We took handfuls of dried morel mushrooms from a coffee can above the refrigerator, quarreling over how many we could stand to give away. I dropped the mushrooms into a baking pan with white wine, where they would gain their moisture back before we sautéed them in butter.

Craig scooped out the insides of a pumpkin from the garden for a pie. He walked to the freezer on the porch and brought back a jar of frozen blueberries. Another pie. He took from the same freezer a jar of cut-up frozen rhubarb. Another pie. The squash from the garden was piled in a cardboard box in the basement. I walked down the stairs into the dark cool, turned on the light, collected four acorn squash, carried them upstairs into the steamy kitchen, peeled off their tough green and orange skins, chopped them, added butter and onions and carrots, and cooked the mixture. And then I puréed it for soup.

We were drinking wine and dancing as we cooked. We were full of joy. We felt generous. To feed all of these people, our friends, with food that we knew in some intimate way, food we had grown or animals we had killed ourselves, was a kind of miracle. The meal we concocted was nearly perverse in its abundance.

Appetizer: venison liver pâté and hot spiced wine.

First course: acorn squash soup, sprinkled with fresh-ground nutmeg.

Second course: spinach and beet green salad with chutney dressing.

Third course: barbecued venison steaks, wild rice, morel mushrooms, buttered beets and honeyed carrots.

Fourth course: roast duck with plum gravy, new potatoes in butter and parsley sauce, and sweet-and-sour cabbage with honey, vinegar and caraway seeds.

Dessert: rhubarb pie, blueberry pie, pumpkin pie. Ice cream.

Then brandy. And coffee. And tea. And as we sat and talked, we ate tart, green and red, thinly sliced apples, slivers of pears, and cheese, and grapes.

In eating these foods — these ducks that we shot out of the sky, that fell, tumbling wing over head, with loud splashes into the cold pond beside our canoe; pumpkin pie that came from a pumpkin that grew all summer long in our backyard garden, surviving three weeks of me cutting open its stalk, scraping out squash borers with the tip of a paring knife; these mushrooms collected over April and May in the just-leafing-out Minnesota woods full of cardinals, scarlet tanagers, bloodroot, new violets, nesting grouse and baby rabbits; this venison, from a big-shouldered spreading-antlered, randy buck Craig killed in November, which we tracked by following the bloody trail it left on bushes and dried grass and leaves — in eating these foods, in this passing of lives into ours, this passing of blood and muscle into our blood and muscle, into our tongues and hearts; in this bridging we were taking up not only food for our bodies, but something that is wild that we wanted for ourselves.

Perhaps it was our own power we were eating. Perhaps it was our own ability to grow, to shoot, to find food for ourselves, that we were eating; our ability to engage creatively with the world. We were eating what we wanted so much. We were eating life.

———————————————

One spring I was walking around Lake of the Isles in Minneapolis with a friend. We were walking fast, dressed in sweatpants and tennis shoes. She would rather have run, but because I was recovering from knee surgery, I could only walk. We took long strides and when I stretched out my leg I could feel the scars there, the manufacturing of new tissue that gave me a strong knee.

We were talking about nothing in particular, about her job as an editor with an agricultural magazine, about running, about lifting weights, about books we had read. Suddenly I shouted, interrupting here, "Look at that!"

She looked to where I was pointing and turned back to see what I was so excited about.

"Look at the ducks," I said. "All those ducks." As we came upon a gaggle of mallards feeding on broken tortilla chips a woman was tossing to them from the grassy bank, I insisted on breaking our stride, stopping to stare.

I was fascinated by the greenheads, how when they moved their heads turned violet and emerald in the light. How there was one duck with a broken bill and a goose with one foot. There was one female among the group of males. Two of the males were chasing her. It was mating season.

My friend had moved on. She talked to me about here lover who teaches writing and literature at a local college. We stopped again because I'd seen a wake in the water, a silvery V streaming out behind a fast-moving muskrat.

"Where?" She squinted.

"There," I said, pointing.

"What is it?"

"A muskrat," I said, watching as it moved toward a small island, its whiskered nose in the air. I notice everything. I hear geese honking outside my window in the middle of the city. I used to track the garter snake in Craig's and my garden from its sunny place in the bean bed to its home under the house, its entryway a piece of bent-up siding. I watch squirrels in the trash cans at the university. I pay attention to spider webs.

I want to know if I can call this love. I want to know if this being aware, this noticing so much, is something I can call love. I want to know how I can say I love the swimming green-heads in Lake of the Isles, when every fall I make an adventure of killing them. I am full of questions. How can I say that killing has anything to do with love? What kind of language do I live in that allows me to embrace this paradox? This tragic conflation of violence and love is part of what I try to resist in the world, yet here I am, in the midst of it.

How is my love for the greenheads, the swimming muskrat, the Canada goose, different from the feelings other hunters have for the animals they kill? Can I have a relationship with those animals alive? Or is the killing, the eating, that magical bridging, a crucial part of my love, part of my relationship with these animals, with the world?

What does it mean, that in my body, helping to keep me alive, to make me joyful, to share joy with people I love, is the breast of a greenhead mallard that I shot down on a cool autumn day and scooped from the cold water with my hand?

*Steve Grooms is a full-time freelance writer liv-
ing in St. Paul, although he hopes to "get a real
job soon," as his daughter attends "a pricey
West Coast college."
Steve lives with his
wife, Kathe, and two
hunting dogs. When
not in St. Paul, they
enjoy spending time at their cabin in the
Apostle Islands area of Lake Superior. Steve's
writing credits include such books as* Return of
the Wolf, Pheasant Hunter's Harvest, Cry of
the Sandhill Crane, The Ones That Got Away,
Bluebirds, *and* Modern Pheasant Hunting. *A
field editor for* Pheasants Forever *magazine, he
has written many magazine articles on upland
hunting. His contribution to* Minnesota Seasons
*is "my attempt to capture the rich and complex
range of emotions involved with upland hunting."*

STEVE GROOMS

Reprinted by permission of the author. This story first appeared in
Shooting Sportsman magazine.

The Deer Shack Walk

STEVE GROOMS

> **What schemes,
> what dreams caused
> some settler to pile
> stone upon stone,
> log upon log,
> at this spot?
> Had he known
> the lake only
> as a source of water,
> or had he used it
> as I now used it,
> to replenish
> a thirsty soul?**

You get to the grouse covert we call the Deer Shack Walk by a trail that slants off the gravel forest road. On your left as you walk in is a vast aspen clear-cut I've been watching for several years, waiting for the moment those popples begin bearing fruit in the form of fantailed grouse. I missed a sucker shot here once, several years before the aspens were cut. That was a grouse my dog stepped on before smelling it, and it would be hard to say which of the three of us was most astonished.

You walk the trail northward, your shadow dancing playfully before you. Here the trail winds past bracken ferns and a copse of scruffy black spruce that should never hold a grouse and only one time did. No need to be alert through this stretch. This is all preamble.

Bending west, the trail drops to a narrow saddle that forms a drawbridge across a long, serpentine swamp ringed by alders and dotted with tamaracks. From this point on, you might flush a grouse anywhere.

Just across the drawbridge lies the dilapidated deer hunter's camp that gave this covert its name. The shack was abandoned decades ago. The roof now lies in the cellar, and the graying walls have slumped under the insistent pressures of time. I have watched these walls caving in gently for years. The whimsical notion once occurred to me that the shack, if it had eyes, might also have noted changes in me over the years I have passed this way: a few more wrinkles, my beard streaking with gray, my step no longer so light. Time slumps us all.

I never pass here without smiling, remembering the first time one of our group came down this trail. The Deer Shack Walk was discovered by Bill Gallea, my longtime outdoor partner and the man who enriched my life by introducing me to grouse hunting.

Bill decided to explore that trail in 1972, a year of spectacular grouse abundance, on a drizzly October day when a ground fog lay all about the low spots like a high school play short on acting but long on dry ice effects. My wife and I recorded the moment on silent Super 8 film: A youthful, hirsute Bill strides up the trail, mugging and waving at the camera, not guessing he was about to discover a grouse hunter's treasure and create a comic legend in the process.

By the time Bill reached the deer shack, he was summoned powerfully by a call of nature that had nothing to do with grouse. That's why Bill was hunkered with his pants around his ankles when the first grouse roared up from the margins of the marsh. It was followed by a second grouse. And a third. A fourth. And a fifth and sixth. And finally (oh sweet agony!) a seventh. Bill could only watch them go as he was armed at the time with a fistful of toilet paper, a short-range weapon.

Our Super 8 film then jump cuts forward in time to Bill's return. He brandishes a brace of grouse, gesticulating vigorously down the trail toward the wonderful new covert he has just discovered, his face radiating joy.

As you stand on the drawbridge studying the old deer shack, your feet mark the convergence of three trails. You must decide: will you walk west, north or southeast?

If you go west, the trail mounts a ridge before entering a mature red pine forest. Here you pass through a place that epitomizes everything grouse habitat should not be. It has no food, no shelter, just a sterile, parklike open woods whose towering conifers keen soulfully in the slightest breeze. In such a place one does not expect grouse. In such a place one might expect a family sitting cross-legged on a blanket, serving lemonade and cherry pie from a wicker basket. Nothing is remotely birdy about this place except the grouse that frequently flush from here. This, perhaps, is part of a grousy joke on me — a human who occasionally presumes to write knowingly about grouse hunting. It is a joke I'm not too stuffy to appreciate.

Curving slightly, the west-running trail narrows as it switchbacks through ground thickly grown up in hazel, aspen, birch and dogwood. This looks like grouse cover, and is. Here I once encountered a hen grouse sitting on the left track of the trail, presenting the beady-eyed profile of all grouse on the ground. Then her topknot rose in alarm, and the tension of the moment increased like a guitar string wound to the breaking point. She flushed. My shot was pure reflex. The grouse crashed down before traveling the three feet between the left and right rut of the trail. My conviction that such a shot is not physically possible is only mildly shaken by the fact I have done it several times.

If, at the crossroads by the drawbridge and the deer shack, you choose to take the north trail, you will encounter different country. This is higher ground that carries a hodgepodge of vegetation. Aspens of several age classes are here, mixed with birches and various conifers, plus the ubiquitous hazel that lies about like coils of concertina wire to consternate hunters.

I cannot describe this country in detail because every time I have hunted here I have been more or less lost. The process always begins when I leave the trail by just a few feet to check out a promising spot, and then spend the better part of an hour finding my way back. It happened again four years ago. I was bulling through the brush, furious with my compass for daring to say that the direction I damn well knew was north was, in its idiot opinion, south. Then — *whoa!* — I saw the deer shack in a place about a mile from where I "knew" it sat. Suddenly the topography of my mind broke free of its moorings and whirled around 180 degrees. I gasped and shook my head until my mental compass settled down with its new bearings. Two miles to the north in another covert, I later learned, my wife was having exactly the same experience at exactly the same moment.

Any grouse I meet here are serendipitous. As I am always lost, I never get to learn which significant little bits of cover produce flushes. Sometimes I fancy I lose my way each time at precisely the same spot, wander precisely the same errant path, and come back to recognizable terrain by precisely the same loopy route. If I keep this up long enough I will wear a new path.

It was here, years ago in that time before I hunted with dogs, that a large red-phased male played peek-a-boo with me for several minutes in some old jack pines. He evidently had a higher opinion of my sportsmanship than is held by some people who know me. The grouse refused to fly, and I refused to ground-swat him as he waddled along, boinking with annoyance, the two of us maneuvering like partners in some ludicrous dance. Then the grouse disappeared. More precisely, he dematerialized. Flabbergasted, I was sure of only three things: the grouse wasn't there anymore, he couldn't have walked away unseen, and he sure as hell hadn't flushed. Another grousy joke.

And if, facing the drawbridge by the deer shack, you choose to go southeast, you will discern the faint ghost of an old trail, a foot trail made by people who now are ghosts, kept open by deer who are not. I had come this way many times before I saw that obscure trail and first ventured down it. Walk softly. There will almost always be birds here, even in low cycle years.

The trail plunges to a spongy strip of land between a pocket marsh and the lake, then ascends a low hill that is so birdy I always approach it thumb-on-safety. Without moving my feet I once shot three grouse here with my side-by-side 20-gauge. Five or six grouse zoomed out of a dogwood thicket, and I downed a double and a late-rising single. Brandy, the gallant springer spaniel who shared fourteen hunting seasons with me, was puzzled: *I've retrieved his "dead bird" twice already, so why's he still yelling at me to go get it?*

From atop the hill you have an exhilarating view of the little lake that, as Thoreau noted of Walden Pond, seems to be a bright blue eye looking straight at heaven. Here I often see ring-necked ducks carving shimmering chevron wakes in the glassy surface of the lake as they distance themselves from me. They needn't worry. I could only get in range by sneaking up on them, and when grouse hunting I refuse to sneak or skulk about. This is a wilderness lake, all property rights currently being held by the porcupines, jays, pine martens, and other creatures who call these hills home. No humans live here.

Someone once did, long ago. Look carefully and you can make out remnants of the foundation of a cabin. It wasn't much of a cabin, but it commanded a view of rare beauty. I stopped here once, years ago, on the first day Brandy and I found the trail that leads to the old cabin. It was an early October day, a Kodachrome day, all sharp edges and saturated color.

And I remember that as the first time I had ever voluntarily paused while hunting. Back in those days, Brandy and I were a pair of grouse-mad hotheads who hunted at the gallop, caroming off trees and reaming paths through the thorn patches, always pressing forward with the desperate velocity of escapees from a chain gang. Brandy worked on the theory that it was her responsibility to flush every grouse in the covert before I could get close enough to do that myself. I would run in the ludicrous effort to arrive at choice bits of cover ahead of my fleet little white dog. Seeing me running, Brandy would just pour on more speed. Thus did Brandy and I chase each other through the October woods, practicing grouse hunting as a contact sport.

Until, as I said, the first day we took the southeast trail and found our way to the hillside overlooking the lake. Grouse were scarce that year. I hadn't fired my gun by the time Brandy and I climbed the hill and studied the abandoned homestead. I sat on a large stump to savor a cigar and let my eyes play over the melange of crimsons, purples, whites and smoky golds reflected on the surface of the lake. The sickly sweet smell of frost-struck ferns lay heavy on the land.

Whatever affected me that day affected Brandy as well. She had never voluntarily ceased her passionate pursuit of grouse long enough to endure fondling from me in the field. Yet on this particular autumn afternoon, Brandy unexpectedly settled beside me and laid a freckled head on my knee. The sweat on my temples turned to chalky salt as I rumpled her ears.

As the glowing ash slowly reduced my cigar, I indulged in woolly speculations about the people who once lived here. A rust-pocked porcelain pail lay on its side near an old shed. Who used to take it down the hill to fetch water? Had this old cabin once witnessed scenes of passion or grief? Did these walls ever shake with the bawl of a newborn? What schemes, what dreams caused some settler to pile stone upon stone, log upon log, at this spot? Had he known the lake only as a source of water, or had he used it as I now used it, to replenish a thirsty soul?

I wanted to believe the old cabin had been the site of romance or tragedy. More likely, of course, its builder was a lanky Norwegian lad just off the boat who was gulled by a land developer into believing wheat would flourish on these piney hills. Or perhaps the cabin was winter shelter to an owly old fur trapper who changed underwear twice a year and brushed his teeth less often than that.

My mind drifted from unknowable matters to eternal questions. I asked myself how I could so eagerly kill grouse while loving them so deeply. Perhaps, I thought, I should hunt without a gun, contenting myself with experiencing the stab of excitement at their thunderous flushes. Catch and release grouse hunting.

Yet I knew that would satisfy me no more than it would satisfy Brandy. For, like Brandy, I want — *really* want — to interrupt those gallant flights, to knock the grouse out of the sky, to possess them. Only, unlike Brandy, I am plagued afterward with hunter's remorse as I regard the limp and frequently disheveled bird in my hand, knowing that my possessing it has deprived the grouse of most of its beauty and the magic spark of life.

Of course, I know the usual arguments. I knew them then and replayed them in my mind that afternoon. How the life of a single fall grouse is highly expendable. How killing one's own food is more honorable than having others do it in windowless buildings under fluorescent lights. How my taking the few birds I am able to hit does no harm to local populations or the race of grouse.

Though true, those arguments have always failed to satisfy me. I love individual grouse, not just grouse as a generality, yet I kill them. Dammit, it feels odd to kill something you love. For some reason, I have never felt that paradox more poignantly than on the afternoon Brandy and I first found the old homestead overlooking the lake.

Then the cigar was gone, and I was no wiser than when I had lit it.

Just south of the old homestead there is a rectangular open space, possibly land once tilled as a garden. I rose and ambled along the rim of the hill through that clearing, Brandy skittering energetically around me. It was no sensible place to go looking for a grouse, but I was not yet ready to abandon my melancholic musings or the sight of the lake.

The grouse was probably as surprised to encounter a hunter so far from a road as Brandy and I were to find a bird in that naked, sunny garden. On throbbing wings it rushed off the hillside directly out over the lake, a large gray-brown *togata* cock bird. He was the only grouse I've ever seen flying absolutely in the open with no intervening veil of brush and no camouflaging background, just a bright, bold bird hurrying into a cloudless sky. And I, by God, *saw* him, saw each feather, saw his iridescent epaulets, saw the gleaming black tail band, saw his dark and luminous eye.

The grouse was high and well out over the water before I fired. At the shot the bird went limp, a puppet with severed strings, falling and falling before plumping down on a tiny island off the southwest shore of the lake. Brandy made the first and only water retrieve of a downed grouse in her long career.

This fall, God willing, I will return to the old deer shack and pause to choose which of the trifurcating trails I should take first. I will, as always, end up walking all three. As always, I'll get lost on the north trail. Sooner or later I will find my way to the hillside over the lake and to the stump by the old cabin foundation.

I will not be alone. Spook will be there, the young English setter who now shares my hours afield. Though Spook has Brandy's white-hot passion for birds, he always has time for interludes of affection. Spook will be pleased to break off hunting long enough for me to squeeze his ears and tell him he is a gentlemen, one hell of a hunting buddy and a credit to the race of setters.

I will be there, a bearded man somewhat past the midpoint of life, an admittedly sentimental man who will be sure to carry a cigar to honor the memory of this spot. And if by the time I reach the stump I have been graced with the gift of a grouse, I will take it out to smooth its plumage and mull again over questions that have no answers but which for that very reason should be confronted from time to time.

Brandy will be there. How could she not be? Though old age and cancer finally doused her fierce flame, I feel her gay spirit everywhere I go. Especially do I feel the nearness of her in places like this where we spent so many happy hours crashing about in our uniquely goofy imitation of grouse hunting.

And in that same sense, the hillside grouse will be there, just as surely as he was on that golden October afternoon fourteen years ago. For out of all the grouse I have known in three decades of hunting them, he was *the* grouse, the bird I watched rushing into an open azure sky, the bird whose memory burns within me with the pure intensity of a laser beam, the bird who died as cleanly as I hope someday to do.

Richard E. Massey, host of Prairie Sportsman *on Public TV, spends his prime time on Lac qui Parle Lake hunting ducks and geese with his boys, Jake and Will. With his wife, Sue, he continues a hundred-year tradition of raising young Masseys on the prairies. Along with his writing and TV work, Richard teaches English at Lac qui Parle Valley High School and holds a chair on the Lac qui Parle Lake Association's Watershed Board. Getting kids interested in hunting, fishing, habitat development, and water quality has always been among his major goals. At present, Richard is concerned about "the growing use of electronics and advanced gadgetry in fishing and hunting." Compound bows and in-line muzzleloaders upset him. He plans to spend time in the near future defending his hobby of darkhouse pike spearing.*

RICHARD E. MASSEY

Old Dogs

R I C H A R D   E .   M A S S E Y

"I could see the sorrow in each man's eyes. None of them wanted to see old Pal go under. Maybe because they were old dogs, too. These men had given me their advice and fellowship since I was little. I could recall sitting atop the shoulders or knees of all these men. I owed them all, and I owed the dog, too. "

The smoke from the old briar pipe curled out and was blown straight sideways by a northern wind that shrieked down the lake. A line of men crouched and watched for ducks on Tennis Shoe Pass, north of my hometown on the prairies of western Minnesota. This pass was actually a country road diked up to cross the lake. Ducks had to pass through on their way up and down it.

Whitecaps hissed against the opposite shoreline across the highway. A line of birds raced down the lake, heading for the pass.

"Mark!" commanded my old man, setting down his pipe and crouching to his knees. All eyes were now on the ducks. It was a duck day on a Minnesota pass. The conditions were excellent for gunning. The big lake was running strong, and a migration of bluebills had just moved in with November. The pass was loaded that day — the duck hunters had moved in along with the ducks. The fall bluebill shoot was always well attended in those days.

It was then possible — indeed, if a man were good, it was probable — to bring home the limit of eighteen divers from that lake, sometimes within two hours. As the line of ducks broke over the pass, guns began to pop. I'll always remember that day for the series of events that began just after those shots.

A big chestnut-colored dog tiptoed across the edge ice that bordered the shoreline, ending forty yards out onto the lake. It was an old dog I knew well, Earl Maher's Pal. Earl was my father's best friend and like a second old man to me. Pal plunged into the open water and began retrieving ducks. A snorting began that I could hear even over the howl of the wind. Earl, my dad and I had driven to the lake in the wee hours of a bone-cold morning, and now, with luck, we could go home with three limits by noon. With luck.

The duck dog was snorting out and back, grabbing ducks, carefully laying each one on the ice shelf before swimming out for more. Time was running short for the old dog, I thought, as two dead ducks drifted away from him down the lake, blown by the wind. From their blinds along shore, all the men could sense something was going wrong for old Pal. He had made the last two retrieves swimming against the current and wind, and it had taken something out of him. He couldn't get up on the ice ledge. Front paws thrown over the shelf ice, he struggled for purchase. Time after time we watched him heave himself up onto the ice, but each time he sank back into the gun-blue water. We all strained with him, muscles tightening. A flock of five ducks sneaked through the pass, but no one was watching. All of us watched the dog. He was hanging there now.

"He'll get his breath and go," yelled my old man to Earl. It seemed as though he might be right. As Pal clung to the ice, I could see his flanks heaving in and out. His plume of frosty breath cooled and whitened his muzzle. One duck in the pile next to him began to kick, its leg slapping the ice, sounding like a baseball card when the spokes of a bicycle hit it. That's what it sounded like to me, anyway. I was that close to childhood.

Men had gathered on the shore with us, across the ice from Pal now, and we slowly began to realize that my old man had not guessed right. Pal was not gathering strength for another spring. Pal was done for. Pal was barely hanging on. He was shaking and shivering. The energy in his old body had been spent retrieving those ducks. He was cold. Cold and old and alone. He was whining, a sound alien to the throat of a proud dog like Pal.

I guess we never forget the day we know for sure we are grown up. I know. I can recall each incident of that whole day. I was weedy in those days, but I was tough. I was puffed up that day: I was sixteen years old, I had a best girl, and I had cracked the starting lineup of the high school football team. I was bruised from the drubbing I had received on the gridiron the night before, but I felt good. The bluebills were in, and I was shooting the pass with the old boys, my pa's bunch.

Not many a grown man would try to gun the pass with those old boys. It was real shooting, you see. This wasn't a deke shoot, where the ducks sail in with their legs down to land. Pass-shooting bluebills in a forty-mile-per-hour wind was the ultimate challenge in those old lead-shot days. I could gun with the best of them, and the old men who stood around me *were* the best. For many hunters, the science of leading a duck tearing across the pass was an unsolvable puzzle, but not to these old ballistics wizards. All of these men had put in at least fifty years with a gun in their hands. Several who stood around me now had chased Pancho Villa down in Mexico with the National Guard.

Now, as I stood with them on the shore, I could see the sorrow in each man's eyes. None of them wanted to see old Pal go under. Maybe because they were old dogs, too. These men had given me their advice and fellowship since I was little. I could recall sitting atop the shoulders or knees of all these men. I owed them all, and I owed the dog, too. He was the dog of my youth, you see. Not my dog, but the dog of my youth. His eyes sagged a little, and his broad back bowed with age. "Not much different than the old boys," I thought. Now a young heart needed to save the dog. I was needed. It was payback time.

"Get a rope!" I yelled, and those old boys snapped into action. They were like old fire horses who jumped at the clang of the bell. It didn't matter that they were almost out to pasture themselves; they rose to the occasion. I watched them moving around me as I pulled off my hippers. They were going to save that old dog whether I helped or not, I knew that. I also knew they realized the advantage my weedy young body had out there on that thin ice.

Pal was still hanging on. He had some purchase with his claws but had slid back a little into the freezing water. He would hold on until he couldn't anymore, but clearly life was slipping away. He knew his time had come. Old muscles fluttered under his oily coat. He called with a trembling voice.

I thought about what it would be like to have to go to sleep that night remembering that call, and I moved. He wasn't going down that day! Yes, I knew what a cold-blooded practical man would do. A practical man would weigh the life of an old worn-down half-blind rat-tailed retriever, and he would snort. I knew that, but Pal wasn't just a bag of bones and hair. I still bear the scars on my rear where he had none too carefully clamped his jaws. I was five years old when he hit the water of Lac qui Parle Creek to save me. Earl had trained him well, and he knew when to act on his own, too. He saw me slide down the bank and into the rain-swollen current. He knew a young child shouldn't be there. His retrieve by the seat of my pants dented my dignity along with my derriere, but saved both. Now I was going to pay him back.

With a rope attached to my ankle, I began my mission. Nails had been dug out of a car trunk. With a twelvepenny in each chopper mitt, I had two ice picks to claw my way over the ice. I moved forward with a sick feeling in my stomach. I knew the ice would be painfully thin and I'd feel a lot older by the time I reached Pal. But it was my choice, and I wanted it. Boys these days run up a high score playing Nintendo. Boys in those days wanted to be outdoorsmen like their fathers.

I set my teeth and kept crawling. The ice cried under my weight, and Pal cried as he saw me coming. Duck hunters know November ice. They've all stretched their luck on it a time or two. Its two-inch thickness supports, but just barely. I was down on my belly, distributing my weight. The one-inch ice ahead of me was a thin white sheet leading into some of the meanest-looking lake water I'd ever seen. My pace wasn't fast. I was snailing along on the treacherous ice. The Arctic-cold wind came tearing up the legs of my pants. Why hadn't I stuffed the cuffs into my wool socks? I stopped to pull my stocking cap down over my ears and looked back for a second at the old boys. They were flapping their arms and stomping around to keep warm there on the shore. Guns down, and ducks, flying all over the place, forgotten now.

I had to set a careful course. "I'll line up off to the side of Pal as I come across," I thought. "He's weakened the ice in front of him, that's plain. Besides, if I'm out here anyway, why not pick up the ducks? Kind of a frosting-on-the-cake routine." Did I really think it would be that easy? Yes. I'd grab the dog by the collar, let him walk back, and fetch those ducks, too.

I slid on, pushing my body with my toes now. I had given up the nails because I would need my hands free. I remember my heart nearly burst just then when an awesome sound assailed my ears: A big flock of bluebills pitched into the open water only ten feet from me. I goggled back at their beady yellow eyes. Close, at eye level, they seemed like an army of alien invaders. They had scared the liver out of me. "Yaah!" I yelled at them. The birds raced away across the surface of the water.

I looked into Pal's eyes and murmured soothingly to him. I wanted to get him ready to go. He mustn't panic and lunge, or we might both be plunged into he water.

"Let's go, old buddy," I whispered as I reached over to grab his collar. I remember thinking at the time how old he had gotten. That bluish-milky cast in his nearly blind eyes shone out at me. He turned his head to face the shore and the old boys. They were yelling encouragement. He seemed to be focused on the sound of their voices, concentrating. As I stretched slowly toward him, his eyes centered and set on me. With a groan of arthritic pain, he lunged for me. I grabbed him by the loose skin on his neck and pulled.

He was out of the water in a bound. His front legs were on my back, and he was using my head as a foothold for one hind leg. I was pushed down into the lake as the thin ice began to give way. Pal ran up and over me. As he dug for shore, my back straightened out and my chest and head bobbed back to the surface. I was soaked, and my clothes began to freeze in an instant. The moment the dog had made contact with the surface ice, however, the old boys had started pulling the rope My chin scraped across the ice as they hauled me in. I didn't have time to be scared. I was flying along across the ice so fast I passed the dog and slid into shore feet-first, like a baseball player.

Greasy fleece-lined storm coats were hastily thrown over dog and boy, and we were hustled into town to get warm. They gave me a belt of brandy, and one of them shoved a cigar into my mouth. It was a time to celebrate. We sat in the back booth of Stan Ronning's cafe, telling stories, staying warm, listening to the drip, drip, drip of my frozen clothes thawing out over the oil burner. It had been quite a day. I knew then, as I dunked my donut into a cup of scalding coffee, that it was a special day, one I would never forget.

Pal? He was none the worse for wear. Like the old boys, he was tasting the tough side of life. He was down, but clearly not out and, like the old boys, he still had a few good years left to shuffle around the duck sloughs.

KENT COWGILL

Kent Cowgill grew up in Silver Creek, Nebraska, a prairie town so tiny he fondly recalls the Homecoming night he played quarterback on the high school football team and, still in pads and helmet, a breathless alto saxophone in the marching band at halftime. Now a professor of English at Winona State University, Kent has published numerous outdoor stories and essays in such magazines as Field & Stream, Fly Rod & Reel *and* Gray's Sporting Journal. *He has also published literary fiction, scholarly essays in a range of academic journals, and two recent books:* Raising Hackles on the Hattie's Fork *(Atlantic Monthly Press, 1990) and a baseball novel,* The Cranberry Trail *(Lone Oak Press, 1996). He lives with wife Jane in Winona, where he remains equally wedded to the region's haunting grouse coverts and trout streams.*

Reprinted by permission of the author. This essay first appeared in *Trout* magazine, published by Trout Unlimited.

Seasons

KENT COWGILL

> " Momentarily
> subdued, the fish
> lies quiet before me,
> a slash of color
> on grass blades
> still glazed by rain.
> It is too perfect,
> this image that
> somehow saddens
> as it thrills.
> Season's end.
> A half-year from
> a new beginning. "

The gravel road bends away from the highway, curls past the rusting cages of an abandoned mink farm, then drops into the valley alongside the streambed. From my car's shrouded interior, I peer apprehensively through the rain-streaked windshield to get a first look at the water. For a week, sodden skies have hung over the Minnesota farmland, unloading periodic showers without moving on, and I tense against the expected sight of a cocoa-colored torrent flecked with foam. But the water is dark, a leaden reflection of the heavens. Though a harrowing west wind rakes the river's surface, my hands relax on the steering wheel. I'll be able to fish.

It is not the ending I would have chosen. In the Closing Day of the Mind, the stream flows out of a languid summer into slanted rays of October light. The fly line unfurls over shards of crystal, the water broken only by a streamside maple's fluttering reds and golds. In the Closing Day of the mind bees drone in terminal blooms of wild aster, hawks trace wide, looping arcs on the thermals, and from dense awnings of shore grass the trout drift lazily toward grasshoppers swept away on a last debauch.

The car rolls on through the drizzle, over a leaf-matted roadbed carpeted by aspen and cottonwood, past farmhouses with smoke billowing from the chimneys, to a pasture gate. A hundred yards beyond rests another farmstead, usually astir with barking dogs and the clank of machinery, now hunkered down quietly in the wind.

The stream lies at the bottom of a cattle path, muddied to mid-ankle by the hooves of the pasture's Holsteins. Bovine myself in heavy sweater and mud-caked hip boots, I cross where they have crossed to the opposite shore. Though the riffle is barely calf-deep, I'm wheezing slightly as I struggle for footing. Is it the boots, so unwieldy after the freedom of a summer spent "wading wet," or the chill whisper of Time? In my vest are the reading glasses to which, after months of vain procrastination, I have recently been forced to surrender. Threading line now through the rod guides, I remember the first intimations of their inevitability: a June dusk, a tiny fly held at arm's length toward the fading light, and a tippet that stubbornly refused to find its way through the eye.

I make three or four false casts, feeding out line. Though wisps of cloud trail so low in the valley it seems I might snag one on a backcast, conditions are moderately improved. The drizzle has stopped, and the wind now rakes up spray only in occasional gusts. On each cast I must *throw* the fly into its buffets, driving the rod hard with my forearm — but if I do it right, waiting an extra half-second for the weighted fly to clear behind me, the line straightens commandingly, and the nymph burrows past my hat brim to the dark water ahead.

For two hours I fish without a strike, often distracted. At the first wooded bend a heron lifts off the water, *skree-skreeing* at its eviction from a choice elbow pool. The leaves of an adjacent cornfield rustle agitatedly, then explode as a huge flock of starlings rise and peel away in the wind, trailing across the valley for a half-minute like tattered shreds of black cloth. A few of my casts bore through to their target. Far more parachute down short amid limp coils of leader. Or shoot long as I overcompensate and snag weeds on the opposite shoreline. Or backlash on the rod guides as I lose tempo in a sudden gust.

I finally lay the rod down. From the shirt pocket beneath my sweater I extract a peanut butter sandwich, squeezed flat as pita bread in its waxed paper, but still dry. The stream's three best pools are behind me, wind-whipped and whiplashed by errant casts and fouled fly line. The hip boots, one with a pinhole leak that has soaked my leg to the knee, drag like cement shoes. Ahead lies a quarter-mile of dead water I've fished without success for years. It is less a pool than a trough, chest-deep but sluggish as a Mississippi bayou. In midsummer a fly alights and expires, inert on the overheated water, while a nymph splashes down ponderously and sinks at once to the mossy muck below.

But this isn't midsummer, I tell myself, finishing the sandwich. The moss is gone, and the water is cold. Analytical or self-deluded, I tie on a black Woolly Worm and resume casting from the shore. The wind, now quartering downstream, drags the weighted fly through the choppy water as it bows the floating line taut. My eyes squint to focus on the tiny knot where the line joins the leader. On the third cast it pauses in mid-drift, or seems to. I set the hook — and haul up from the depths a waterlogged willow. Still, I have a heightened sense of possibilities. Except when the hardest gusts send it skittering wildly across the water, the line hugs the surface in a satisfying big-bellied arc, pulling the sunken nymph behind it at a tempting creep.

I fish slowly on, my eyes so intent on the knot they begin to tear. Again comes the pause, almost imperceptible in the chop, and I strike once more. This time the line throbs, the rod arches, and the belly of a hooked fish flashes faintly on the bottom. Five minutes later the trout lies on the grass at my feet, a fat female of about seventeen inches, her golden pectoral fins edged with ivory and her sides dappled in orange and red.

Momentarily subdued, the fish lies quiet before me, a slash of color on grass blades still glazed by rain. It is too perfect, this image that somehow saddens as it thrills. Season's end. A half-year from a new beginning.

Again, I look hard at the trout. Hauled from the freezer in the grim depths of a Minnesota winter, the ice-sheath would melt, and the dead, hoarfrosted flesh would thaw, transmuted once again into gold. A kind of alchemy. For a long moment I want the fish with an intensity beyond fathoming.

Then, as suddenly as it came, the moment passes. When I remove the hook, the fish flops heavily toward the water, her belly sagging with the eggsacs that would burst from a knife-slit like glowing embers. Upstream, in the woods beyond the next fenceline, there lie pools I've never cast into. If the season's few remaining hours offer up a last trout or two in the gathering winds of autumn, I'll keep them for that mid-winter meal — a couple of ten-inchers to serve with a good, dry Riesling.

But not this one.

WINTER All around

us this sparkling snow stretches.
Here and there a few shore lights
bloom like pale moons on the
horizon of an ice planet.
The snow shifts, the wind pulling
it first one way, then another,
making a ridge here, a curve there,
a landscape architect shaping
this frost-bound desert.

RICHARD BEHM
From Of Ice Deserts, Eelpout and Men

November

LARRY M. GAVIN

Bluebills pile up

On Tim's slough

And the weather man,

More lost than is normal,

Says rain, sunshine, snow.

But we know, the dog and I

That city weather does not apply here,

In cattails under darkening sky.

These ducks have flown so far

Ahead of this wind

They feel they own it,

And by association

Own the open water

A kind of unmanageable daughter,

Needing their attention

So they land,

Ending the way they began.

Behind them snow starts.

Delicately at first

A portent

A sign

A drifting lacy reminder

That supper is cooking,

And that these days

Darkness

Always arrives

Faster than light.

Published by permission of the author.
This poem first appeared in *Gray's Sporting Journal*.

ROBERT TREUER

Robert Treuer is a writer and tree farmer near Bemidji, Minn. His published works are The Tree Farm *(Hungry Mind Press, originally published by Little Brown),* Voyageur Country *(University of Minnesota Press),* and A Northwoods Window *(Voyageur Press). His short stories and articles have appeared in* Atlantic, Yankee, Washingtonian *and other publications, and he has written more than six hundred newspaper essays. Born in Vienna, Austria, he was separated from his parents as a boy escaping the Holocaust but later reunited with them. He served in the Army in World War II. He worked for ten years as a labor paper editor and union organizer in Wisconsin before moving to his Minnesota home on what was then an abandoned farm. He taught high school, college and adult classes, and became a community organizer on Indian reservations. After working for the U.S. government in Washington, D.C., for most of the 1970s, he returned to Minnesota to resume writing, tree farming and teaching. He has six sons and one daughter.*

From the book, *A Northwoods Window,* published by Voyageur Press. Reprinted by permission of the author.

My Dear Hunter

ROBERT TREUER

" It is a fairly hard walk that I take, but I know the terrain well. Shortly before meeting Peggy I hear her shoot, then again. I freeze, listen, wait, give her a few minutes, then go to meet her. "

"Tomorrow," says Peggy, "we have a babysitter and we can both go deer hunting."

We like to hunt quietly, meandering through the woods, standing, walking softly, mindful of the wind and the way the deer tend to travel.

"I'll go around the spruce hill and skirt the swamp. Come out just past the white pine hit by lightning."

"Give me a few minutes to mosey around. I'll be waiting up that hill, where the red-tailed hawk had her nest. Ten minutes."

Then there are times when we are off in different directions by mutual consent, hunting privately, a very comfortable way of doing things that suits our preferences. But it does not work all of the time. This year seems to have been jinxed.

"Where were you?" I ask her back at the house. "I cut through the tag alder swamp and across the ridge and came out right where you said you'd be!"

I am miffed, having been stood up, having made the arduous walk for naught. One never surprises a deer going through that swamp; it is too noisy. The only time I've seen a deer there was when a group of does about ran me down, being chased by an amorous buck, and that was a few years ago.

"I got cold. And hungry," she says.

"You came in the house with shoes on," son Tony upbraids me.

"Five sticks of wood, Dad," Davis adds. It is the standard penalty.

"I made that long drive all for nothing," I protest. "Five deer could have walked right past your stand."

In fact I had seen no fresh tracks when I came out, but righteous indignation is sufficient grounds for a little prevarication.

"You've got to bring in five sticks of firewood," Tony insists. The customary ingress for family members is through the mud room, where one changes to slippers, and thence into the main part of the house.

Peggy is avoiding my glare, pretending great interest in her steaming bowl of soup and the daily newspaper.

"You mean you haven't even seen one?" she asks several days later, the deer season near its end. "All that time out in the woods and you haven't even seen one?" There is an aura of complaint, of fault-finding in her tone of voice. She is begrudging me the time in the woods while she has to go to town to work.

"You can use my rifle and try your luck," I tell her.

"I will," she says, still a bit harsh, belligerent.

She bundles, wraps, bundles up some more, my sylphlike spouse looking like a candidate for Weight Watchers as she rolls out the door.

"That rifle of yours weighs a ton," she complains. "It's a blunderbuss, a cannon."

"Blundercuss, blundercuss," says Megan, and Micah echoes her, in love with the sound of the word as Peggy disappears among the trees and I am left watching the children. It is a perfect day for the kind of hunting we like. Not too terribly cold, but the wind is gusting and there is a flurry of alternating sleet and snow in the air. Good for tracking, for silent travel. But I wish I were going out instead of Peggy as the twins clamor and Tony and David engage in another of their endless disputes.

"Well?" I ask hours later as Peggy returns.

"Well what?" she snaps.

"Did you at least see one?"

"I stepped on one."

"You did what?"

"Big doe. I was following the main runway below the crest of the long hill, and I thought that lump forty feet down looked like ears. But it just couldn't be a deer sleeping right in the path. So I kept going. It was sleeting awfully hard. I looked again and thought it looked suspiciously like a sleeping deer, but who ever heard of one sleeping with you so close. Then when I stepped over the fallen jack pine, it stood up. My, it was big."

"Did you shoot? Did you hit it?"

There is a long silence. "I couldn't get the safety off," she finally says. "That is an awful gun. I don't see how you put up with it all these years."

It is the last weekend of the season. I still have seen nothing.

"But you've been out there from daybreak to nightfall," Peggy reminds me, the complaint evident in her voice.

"Aaarrrgh."

"Daddy said aaarrrgh," Micah points out. "Aaarrrgh."

Peggy and I team up. A lovely early winter day, brisk, windy, not too cold, with a trace of snow on the ground. A few minutes into the forest there are tracks all around. Several deer have been feeding during the night and are probably bedded nearby. We split, agreeing to rendezvous a few minutes later at the opposite end of the ridge, each of us taking one side of the hill.

I see lots of deer sign on the way, but no deer. Peggy is waiting for me at the end of the walk.

"A big buck was watching me as I came over the top," she says. "He just trotted away. I couldn't get a shot at him."

What can I say? We agree she will circle and take a stand nearly half a mile away on the next hill, overlooking the brushy marsh. I will circle the other way, walking fairly slow-ly, but not too quietly. Deer will usually stay up to a quarter-mile ahead, and the plan is for me to drive them toward Peggy.

"You've got ten minutes' head start," I say as we part.

It is a fairly hard walk that I take, but I know the terrain well. Shortly before meeting Peggy I hear her shoot, then again. I freeze, listen, wait, give her a few minutes, then go to meet her.

"Two," she says, breathing hard.

"Where are they?" I glance about for the carcasses.

"I don't know. The buck came walking out and I shot, so he stopped and stood there. Then the gun jammed. Then I shot again and he walked about ten feet and disappeared."

We search, but there is no blood, no sign of a hit, just foot-prints of two deer running fast. We agree to go our separate ways.

The season ends for me as it has gone throughout. I see nothing. Peggy avoids my eyes as she comes in.

"Saw another one," she finally admits. "I was climbing the fence over by the northwest corner and it got up."

"How far away?" I'm not sure I want to hear this.

"About ten feet."

"Why didn't you shoot?"

"I'd leaned the gun against the fence post."

"We'll be eating venison after all," I announce two days later.

"But Dad, the season's over," says David.

"Got one on the way into town this morning." They are amazed: Daddy is a poacher; my husband, the criminal. I enjoy being taciturn, munching my supper. Then I relent.

"It ran into the side of my truck. I called the game warden and he gave me a permit to keep it."

ROD DIMICH

Rod Dimich, an avid hunter and fisherman, lives with his wife and three children ten miles north of Grand Rapids, Minn. In his writing, he tries to search for the feelings people experience while hunting, fishing, camping or scouting. Rod is one of the founders of the Minnesota Deer Hunters Association and co-creator of that group's quarterly magazine, Whitetales, *in which the accompanying story first appeared. He still edits the magazine. He also teaches English and journalism at Grand Rapids High School, enjoys his family, and is "constantly amazed at the beauty and spirituality of the great outdoors."*

The Outpost Expedition

ROD DIMICH

> **All the while, the snow fell, but we did not notice. Somewhere, deer hunters were in camp, laughing and lamenting. Somewhere, deer and grouse and other woodland creatures were playing out their games of survival. But here, on the Outpost Island, two young boys were becoming men.**

One snowy November night many Novembers ago, two young men came of age on a balsam-birch island in the Big Swamp. That island was known to members of the Big Swamp Camp as The Outpost, and for good reasons. First, it was on the outer limits of the traditional Big Swamp hunting territory, bordering on a new frontier, a remote area where only foolish or lost hunters ventured. And second, to go there, without even requiring a vote by the Big Swamp Camp, was on the outer limits of good sense.

These two reasons were enough for my teenage partner in adolescent bumblings, the venerable, venturesome, and verbose self-proclaimed Prince of the Big Swamp, Bobby "The Buckman" Bilkovich, to enact the "Let's do it" rule of youth. The elderly portion of the BSC, according to Buck and me, consisted of anyone over age twenty-one and married. The married part was the key, we kept telling them, for that was what turned Saturday nights into Monday nights. We knew it all. Anything the older vets would tell us, we either knew already or could add to. Oh, the power and intellect of youth.

What precipitated the Outpost Expedition was a kitchen table foray after a couple of "no deer sighted" days. The red-clad players of this November drama had the think tank filled with theory, ideology and deer-county dogma. We discussed every possible solution to the deerless dilemma.

The Outpost Expedition started with the big mouth of "Buckman" who, in a typical manner, without thinking, spouted off about the old guys hanging around the camp too much, afraid of gallivanting as they had in their younger days, being static in their ways, being just as comfortable in the camp's closer confines as they were each Saturday night watching Lawrence Welk. Their response was more a challenge than an answer: "If you and your partner in mouth know the whereabouts of our missing deer herd, just maybe you twin Deerslayers might head up to The Outpost and muster up something for the meat pole."

The Outpost was the ultimate challenge. Two miles of hard swamp, wet and tangled, lay between the camp and the island. There was virtually no way in from other areas. I was willing to eat some crow, compliment Lawrence Welk, and even offer to mosey around the next day to stir up some deer, but Buck had other thoughts.

"Good idea," Buck roared, much to the Swampers' delight and my horror. "We'll even go one better. We'll camp there so as not to disrupt the early morning flight."

I couldn't believe my ears. Not only hunt the Outpost, but camp there? That was what the veterans called "whiskey talk," though we weren't old enough to drink. We were sunk. There was no way we could get out of this one. I shot a good, solid stare at Buck. And when he sent back a nod and that smirk that said, "We'll show 'em," my sense of dread deepened.

Buck and I spent the rest of the night planning and packing. The Big Swampers, meanwhile, busied themselves revelling in the mere mention of the prefix "out," laughing hysterically at comments like, "I'm going to the Outpost, er, I mean the outhouse." So it went, on through breakfast, even at our departure.

The Outpost Expedition had to pay off for us. Years of chiding were at stake. We left that morning, laden like pack mules with camping gear and food. We were missing one important ingredient for this hunting stew: a tent. Buck shrugged this off: "Even if we had one, I wouldn't take it. Tents are for swamp greenhorns. We're born and bred swampers."

The path (figuratively speaking, for there was nothing of the sort through that jungle) was as difficult as always. And, as always, the swamp took me in. Impassable as it was, this basin of tannin-stained water, nondescript brown wild hay, and drab gray alders held a certain intrinsic beauty, a prevailing presence of primordial creation and humility. The Big Swamp exists entirely unto itself, by itself, and for those who need it for survival or introspection. But now was not the time to wax philosophical. We were on a mission.

And what a mission. Buck forged ahead like a man possessed. Deer sign was minimal. In fact, the farther we delved into the swamp, the less sign we found. I pointed this out to Buck several times, but my words were like a few raindrops in a downpour. The Buckman was Outpost bound. We had walked the first half-hour in darkness, the second in a time when night and day were at odds. We had spoken very little, stopped only twice. When we reached the island, daylight was in full control. A fading moon hung over the island's greenish-white blend of balsam and birch. Formally attired chickadees flitted to and fro. A rusty red squirrel reprimanded everything in sight, and a long flock of geese pencil-lined its way across the ever-brightening morning sky.

We stopped at the first high ground, relieved to step on dry soil. The island was a natural anomaly, a green and ivory emerald in a gray-brown setting. From its highest vantage point, about ten feet, we could see nothing but tag alder tips and several watchtower tamaracks. Two miles southeast was the Big Swamp Camp's high ground. In every other direction, higher ground was farther away, less identifiable. There was little wonder how this solitary island got its name.

Over a cup of coffee, Buck and I went over plans. Nothing was to change. We would go along with what we had decided last night. We would leave the gear here and still-hunt the island until noon, he going west, I east. At noon, we would meet on the island's north side, just south of the windfalls, and decide where to camp. Actually, we were fairly familiar with the island. We had been here quite a few times for spring and post-season scouting, always looking for that elusive edge in search of big bucks. Still, we had never hunted here. Others had, but sparingly. The effort to get here, and then the dreaded drag, were just too much. Besides, we had plenty of deer within reasonable distances of the BSC.

Like a good dog on his first hunt, I sneaked and stopped my way around the island. The going was dreamlike compared to the swamp trek. There wasn't much deer sign, though there was plenty of wolf action. Padded trails as opposed to indented ones are tell-tale indicators. Add to this wolf droppings, and the picture was complete. The island was so remote it was a wolf stomping ground. Deer would be hard to come by. Nevertheless, the hunt was well worth it. This was a land free from the trammels of humanity. No hunters, no vehicles, not even vehicle sounds. Nothing but the winds of wildness and the spirit of the swamp.

When we met at noon, Buck and I shared similar stories. No deer, no deer sign, lots of wolf sign, and considerable doubt about the success of our venture. Buck had, however, found the remnants of an old camp, complete with a newly added blown-over balsam, which we could persuade into a makeshift shelter, as it had perched itself over a couple of springy birch. We then bee-lined for our gear and headed out to our remote camp.

There are few things of more pure delight than setting up camp in the wilderness. The interdependence of task, the meshing of talents, the cooperative nature belie the notion that work must be something dreary, something contrary to play. After an hour, our camp became much more than a place in the woods, a temporary substitute for the comforts of our real camp. It became a personal accomplishment, a sanctuary for survival, a testimonial to the will of the hunter, a monument to the ingenuity of the Big Swamper.

After two hours, we had the lean-to finished. A layer of plastic covered the blown-down balsam. Another layer of balsam branches covered that. Inside, on the moist ground, we laid a carpet of balsam branches. In front, we knocked over some old stumps and banked a good fire. To the left of the fire, we put our woodpile, bow saw cut and hatchet split. Over the fire we put our grill, on which we would broil steaks (nothing but the best for this short crew) and boil water (which we had packed in) for soup and coffee. By the time we were finished, November afternoon shadows were edging in. It was time for the evening hunt.

We each went to spots we had found during our morning hunts. The air had become heavier by then, and a thick cloud mass had settled over the swamp. I knew what that meant. Snow was definitely not part of our game plan. My time on stand went quickly. It was eerily quiet, even the birds of dusk nonexistent. Only an owl's faraway hoot broke the calm. When the first snowflakes began to fall, I headed for camp, even though there was still a good twenty minutes of shooting time left. I did not want to be caught in a whiteout. By the time I got back, silver-dollar-sized flakes were floating down. Buck was there, piling more wood on the fire. All our gear was already under the lean-to. He, too, had seen and heard nothing.

As we readied for supper, more snow fell. The flakes seemed much closer together, so much so that now, rather than distinguishing each flake as a silver dollar, it was more accurate to describe the scene as pitch white. Inside, the shelter was dry and warm. The fire was set just right, the heat welling into us and the smoke going straight up. Our steaks were great, the chicken soup piping hot, the coffee strong and black. Buck and I had never had a meal quite like that one.

After supper, we piled in more wood, perhaps enough for several days, in fact. Why, I am not sure. Maybe we felt secure knowing we would have enough in case we were really snowbound, or maybe it was just that working took our minds off the incredible quiet and isolation. I am sure it was well after ten o'clock when we turned in.

The snow was now at least four inches on the level, but our lean-to was solid, our fire still roaring. The view from inside was amazing. Sparks from the fire reached into the black and snowflake night, an extraordinary blend of orange, white and black, of warm and cold, of opposing forces colliding in a maelstrom of certainty and uncertainty, of reality and spirituality, of life and whatever.

Buck and I talked as never before. We talked of our families, the happiness and the tragedy. We talked of young love, mostly unrequited. We talked of hopes and dreams, what we wanted and what we didn't. We shared secrets, never-before-mentioned hurts, poignant moments, embarrassing times, winning times. It was amazing how close we had been, without realizing it. It was also amazing how similar were the crosses we bore.

All the while, the snow fell, but we did not notice. We were in our own world, a world we had never been in before, a world not only exciting but meaningful, deep and far-ranging. Somewhere, people were in homes, warm and secure. Somewhere deer hunters were in camp, laughing and lamenting. Somewhere, deer and grouse and other woodland creatures were playing out their games of survival. But here, on the Outpost Island, two young boys were becoming men.

When we fell asleep I am not sure. When we awoke and looked at our watches at five o'clock, all we knew was that the night had been unbelievably eventful and that neither of us had ever slept so well. We made coffee and oatmeal over the early morning deer-season fire and gazed into the still-dark sky. The moon was bright, and millions of snowflakes on the ground matched the stars in the sky. We stirred the fire occasionally, adding our own orange sparkles to the show. We ate and got ready for the morning hunt, agreeing to hunt only two hours, then break camp and get back to the Big Swamp Camp by noon.

The morning hunt went as expected. We knew there were no deer here and set our expectations accordingly. After two hours, we headed back to civilization, through six inches of snow. The journey through the swamp was totally different from our pilgrimage of the day before. We were going back unsuccessful as deer hunters, but victorious in a way we had not expected. As we neared the main trail heading back to the camp, Buck turned to me and asked in a voice I could relate to, "What do we tell them? The truth? Or what they expect us to tell them — a bunch of wild deer stories?"

We both knew the answer and, strangely enough, we somehow knew that they would know, that they had at some time gone through this same sort of awakening. When we hit the Big Swamp Camp, we were greeted by drag marks in the snow. The guys had connected. Ordinarily, we would have been taken aback. They had one-upped us again. Only this time, we were elated. We would take what was coming to use. We had bragged, we had belittled. Now we would admit our failure and acquiesce to our betters or, as we now realized, our brothers of the hunt.

As we followed the drag trail, we smiled, we laughed, and were abjectly glad they had scored. But we were not ready for what greeted us when we reached the woodline. There, under the shadowy balsams, lay two bruiser bucks, an eight- and a nine-pointer. On the rack of the nine-pointer was a note.

Saw two, got same.
If you of Outpost Expedition got one,
come and get us, we will drag same.
If not, drag these.
We'll have lunch, or supper,
as the case may be.

Buck and I looked at each other, smiled, shook hands and said simultaneously, "Let's do it, Big Swamper."

*Peter M. Leschak has been a freelance writer
since 1982, and more than two hundred of his
pieces — features, essays, reviews, short fiction,
poetry, political
analysis and satire
— have appeared
in sixty-two peri-
odicals. A resident
of Side Lake, Minn., he has also written six
books. In addition, more than a thousand of his
photos have been published in newspapers,
magazines, annual reports and brochures. In
summer, Peter moonlights as a smoke jumper,
battling forest fires.*

PETER M.
LESCHAK

This essay previously appeared in *Minnesota Monthly* (1988) and in
The Bear Guardian, North Star Press (1990). Reprinted by permission
of the author and North Star Press.

Night Ski

PETER M. LESCHAK

" Here is the real
sensation of flight —
that I'm swooping
and soaring over
the treetops, that
these sharp-edged
shadows of the
aspens are the trees
themselves.
They whip by, below
and all around, and
the closed-in black-
and-white world
fosters an illusion of
breathtaking speed. "

This may be as close as I come to being a hawk, a nighthawk. I'm riding the snow, but it doesn't feel like it. My skis are as light as sound waves; as buoyant as tail feathers, and almost as quiet. An owl could hear me from a long way off, but only because the night is so still.

Here at the start, the trail is wide, and I have room to skate, pushing from edge to edge in long, flowing sweeps of skis and poles, as if side-slipping in wind. There's a slight crunch to the snow, but it's a smooth noise, like rough air on raven wings.

The forest is awash with moonlight. The bright, full orb is arcing high, nearing the zenith. The shadows of trees are starkly projected onto the snow. The light is hard, and the images are perfect. Each branch and twig is reproduced in fine detail, and the intricate tracery of the forest canopy is there beneath my ski tips. Here is the real sensation of flight — that I'm swooping and soaring over the treetops, that these sharp-edged shadows of the aspens are the trees themselves. They whip by, below and all around, and the closed-in black-and-white world fosters an illusion of breathtaking speed.

Above, the constellations have been polished by moonglow; only the brightest stars are visible. In Orion, Betelgeuse is a fiery red, Rigel a coruscating blue. The trail turns north, and I can see the cup of the Big Dipper rising beyond the woods ahead. Off to the right, blinking between the boughs of pines, is brilliant Capella. The silhouettes of the trees are utterly black, and by contrast the moonlit sky is a dark, translucent shade of blue. It is the color of infinity.

Even though the sun has been down for three hours, it's twenty-nine degrees — in January! (Twenty-nine below would have been closer to the norm.) I revel in this gift of a "subtropical" anomaly. The air is breathable and smells of cold crystal and pine needles. As it rushes past my face it feels cleansing and fresh — vernal air without that brittle Arctic edge.

I hit the crest of the first hill and snowplow just a little. In daylight, I would pole halfway down, digging for velocity. But at night it looks different; the bottom is indistinct, and the bordering trees seem to hem it in. There's a wide curve at the base, and I sail into it — knees bent, poles tucked — like the nadir of a raptor's dive.

I ease into a rhythmic, floating glide, cruising the flats and whisking down slopes. Soon there's a stand of mature aspen, huge trees whose branches are concentrated in distant, lofty clumps. Here are only the shadows of arrow-straight trunks, a whole corridor of thick black striations on the snow, like a gigantic spectrum of some mysterious star. As I race over them it's as if I'm flying past a picket fence, eyes winking in and out of bands of light.

And then I plunge into a dense bower of Norway pines. The track is invisible, absorbed into the murky umbra of deep, tangled woods. I feel my way along the track, tunneling through the blackness and focused on the bright snowfield beyond. It's a galaxy of crystalline sparkles — multicolored pinpoints of moonlight. I burst into their midst, bedazzled by the sky come to earth. The snow is like a thick carpet of rhinestones.

At the halfway point there's a small clearing at the top of a hill, and I pause for a few moments next to a coppice of birches. Their paper bark is as white as the snow, and my eye follows the ghostly trunks upward. A bank of thin cirrus clouds is drifting past, a white swath of milky fleece. In the dimness of the night the birches seem to form a frosty, two-dimensional link between land and sky — between pure snow and pure cloud — different manifestations of water and ice.

The clouds graze the moon and then briefly envelop it. A reddish halo forms and spreads out through the vapor, like concentric waves in a quiet pool. This January cycle of phases is the Wolf Moon, and yesterday we heard a pack singing just before and after sunset, as the moon was climbing out of bluish eastern haze. I would love to hear the wolf pack now.

My breath rises and forms a second halo, a pale aura wreathing my head. The sky is framed by the naked limbs of a maple tree, and my exhalations seem to curl among the branches before dissipating into the molecular ambience and rejoining the atmosphere of the planet. For a moment the cosmos is compressed, and I blow a breath at the moon. It doesn't appear to be that far beyond the top of the maple. A nighthawk could circle it. But the illusion is fleeting. This moon is far and high; it will trek with the stars until past dawn, perched between Auriga and Orion.

I shove off down the rise, gliding into a winding flat stretch that leads to the crest of the Roller Coaster. It's two hills in one. The first slope is a steep curve. You must bank sharply to the right, and just as you straighten out, you shoot up the flank of the ridge. There's another curve at the top, and you slide into it at speed, pivoting a little to aim your skis down the second drop. You make one quick stab with the poles and then tuck in and plummet, flashing through a grove of young aspens. When the trails are icy, it's a harrowing, ski-threatening (and bone-threatening) run.

Tonight the snow is soft, but the Roller Coaster is dappled with blackness, deceptively lit. The moonbeams have modified its figuration. I'm going too fast when I hit the first curve — or that's what it feels like. I overcompensate, confused by the lunar radiation and how it has blended the darkness and light. I skid up the ridge off balance, fighting for equilibrium as I break over the top. Before I hit the trees, I sink into a crouch while making a little jump to the left. The skis slap the snow and grip, and as I start to hurtle down the second slope I feel stable and plumb. I just hang on until the aspens stop streaking past.

If someone were behind me I'd turn back and laugh, sharing the joy of evasion and escape. But I've chosen solitude this evening, and the sound of only one pair of skis. I must smile just to myself, but I don't regret the privacy. Often it's satisfying to feel remote, to be deliciously alone with the moon. You may listen, uninterrupted, to the shadows on the snow, or the spaces between the stars.

In a minute I'm back into the tempo of the trail, weaving through the forest, an apparition flitting between the trees. Suddenly I feel watched. I perceive being the object of attention. Though if there are a pair of eyes upon, me, they don't see much — a brief glimpse of swinging arms, a wavering trail of vapor. I have a sense of being airy, transitory. And yes, there *are* eyes out there; I know it. But I don't feel menaced; I feel escorted. Some nocturnal sentinel is noting my swift passing through the winter woods. A wolf? A fox? An owl? But the eyes feel neither wary nor alarmed. Perhaps it is only God. Surely God is near on a night like this.

Richard Behm is a graduate of what is now the University of St. Thomas. Since living in Minnesota full time as a student, he has

RICHARD
BEHM

returned often, canoeing the Boundary Waters annually with his wife, Mary, and Minnesotan friends, and also visiting "to fish Mille Lacs, to canoe the Rum, and to revel in the state's many treasures." Richard divides up the world by drawing a line through Escanaba, Mich., through Rhinelander and Rice Lake, Wis., then on through Cambridge and St. Cloud, Minn. "Everything above this line is the Northwoods, everything below is someplace else." He is a professor of English at the University of Wisconsin-Stevens Point and a widely published writer whose works have appeared in Sporting Classics, Gray's Sporting Journal, Sports Afield, Field & Stream, *and other publications.*

Of Ice Deserts, Eelpout, and Men

RICHARD BEHM

> **Walleye and eelpout swim in the same water, and with them we, too, swim in that greater, mysterious water, all flesh conjured from star-stuff. Yet the walleye is prized and the eelpout despised. By what standard dare we judge nature?**

It is cold. The three words must suffice as all attempts at metaphor fail. It is as cold as ... and the sentence ends like a trail at the edge of an ice crevice. Just the facts, ma'am. Twenty-nine below. The wind from the north blasting at up to forty miles an hour. The wind-chill eighty or more below — a typical winter night out on the great, shallow, glacial basin of Mille Lacs in northern Minnesota.

Tom, a friend of twenty-five years, and I fish a rocky reef called Sloppy Joe's. Ice shanties cluster like tents around desert springs on other reefs and mud flats across this hundred-thousand-acre lake. A few well-padded and perhaps well-liquored souls (never mind that alcohol is no defense against the cold; myth and custom are almost always stronger than science) jig in holes outside their shanties. They perform that peculiar dance, the Arctic Polka: Lift the left foot, stomp it down. Lift the right foot, stomp it down. Hug yourself and whirl around. In vain they seek to shake blood into numb extremities.

We are fishing in eighteen feet of water and are 2.8 miles from the pine-rimmed shore. We have been here since 3:07 p.m., and it is now past 10:15. We have caught one eight-inch perch and four eelpout, the largest nineteen inches long.

We are in an 8- by 12-foot shelter of insulated particle board, one of a half-dozen such shacks scattered here. There are three windows and a door that closes tight against the explosive winds and drifting snow. There are two bunks made of rough 2 x 4s and two inches of foam. There is a small table and a tin box for a stove that must be continually fed small pieces of oak and fragrant apple wood that we have brought with us. A Coleman lantern swings overhead, casting circles of yellow light and shadowy streaks around the walls. A rust-colored indoor-outdoor carpet covers the floor, except for the corners where four eight-inch holes have been augured. The holes are black eyes rimmed with blue ice, openings into another world.

The ice here is seventeen inches thick, topped by two feet of snow, more where it has drifted or been plowed into piles. The ice is whimsically described as "driveable." And it generally is, though early winter adventurers, anxious to tie into the best fishing, sometimes lose vehicles through the ice. Even now the lake will sometimes crack open like the San Andreas fault and swallow $25,000 worth of fully equipped Cherokee, while the drenched occupants cling to the edge of the crevice. And sometimes the occupants go down with the ship.

We have driven out in Tom's seventeen-year-old Hornet, whose body he has patched repeatedly with flattened coffee cans and layers of gray putty. It's a classic fishing car, having over years of abuse developed an immunity to radiator-hose-eating porcupines, nose-deep muck holes, and, we hope, unexpected ice fissures. Following the plowed road barely marked by wooden poles with bits of blue rag attached, we find one place where the ice has split open and boards have been placed across six feet of open water. On Mille Lacs, they call this flimsy arrangement a "bridge." We peer briefly down into the black and watery gorge, then inch across while the planks bend and creak beneath us. We wonder aloud and laugh about finding our way back across in the dark.

And darkness comes early. Driving out, the air was winter blue, diamond hard, the kind of air that suggests you could take a nine-pound sledge, strike it against the sky, and set the whole universe ringing like a crystal bell. The sun burned westward a brief, pale yellow before succumbing. For a few minutes a line of orange-gold flamed with a field of lavender above, a field of white below. Then it winked out, and the darkness settled down.

Ostensibly we are here for walleye, the Calvin Klein of Minnesota fishing. In Minnesota, some claim there are two kinds of fisherman: walleye fishermen and "trash-fish" fishermen. I once made the mistake of inviting one of these mono-maniacal purists to go along on a spring trout-fishing expedition. He declined, sarcastically noting that he "didn't eat rough fish."

But we have caught no walleyes, nor do we really expect to anymore. Instead we haul up those bottom-dwellers, the ubiquitous eelpout, one of the homeliest creatures God has seen fit to grace the earth with. Though the eelpout — its real name is burbot — is actually a species of freshwater cod and by the accounts of those who have braved its surly countenance a very tasty fillet (James Beard even provides a recipe for it in his fish cookbook), it is universally despised. The ice is usually littered with their carcasses.

It was just a year before, on a sunny Sunday afternoon, with the temperature a tropical five below and the fishing every bit as slow, that Tom and I contrived a game: the first and only eelpout Olympics. The events included the eelpout throw, the eelpout kick, the eelpout home-run derby, and a rousing match of eelpout hockey. Boredom, silliness, whatever its cause, we laughed so hard we could hardly stand up, laughed the way children do who find the world gone suddenly crazy in ways they can explain to no one.

The eelpout, sometimes called a miece-eye, for reasons unclear to me except that the fish does have a decidedly rodent-like face, is ugly. Its face has the charm of a rat's, its body the twisting muscle of a serpent. Long eelpout will wrap around your arm as you extract the hook from their mouths. Couple these less than endearing characteristics with the fact that they are as slimy as a bar floor at closing time, and you can understand why the fish is under-appreciated. It is not unusual to hear a whoop from the inside of a fish-house, shortly followed by a stream of ear-thawing curses and a banging door. Another eelpout is flung into the night to die.

It raises, of course, some disturbing questions. Most of us do eat fish just (well, almost) as ugly as the eelpout. Flounder in the raw only a mother flounder could love; catfish share some of the eelpout's repulsive features; and the case can be made that even the cherished walleye, with its strange, glazed look, would be more appealing as a subject to Diane Arbus than to Michelangelo.

There's a philosophical question raised by the eelpout, a question that has less to do with the nature of beauty than with the nature of ugliness; not why do we raise up one thing and proclaim it beautiful, worthy; but by what right do we cast another down and name it ugly, inedible, unworthy? Walleye and eelpout swim in the same water, and with them we, too, swim in that greater, mysterious water, all flesh conjured from star-stuff. Yet the walleye is prized and the eelpout despised. By what standard dare we judge nature?

It's easy to wax philosophical as this night I watch an eelpout die in the star-glittered snow. All around us this sparkling snow stretches. Here and there a few shore lights bloom like pale moons on the horizon of an ice planet. The snow shifts, the wind pulling it first one way, then another, making a ridge here, a curve there, a landscape architect shaping this frost-bound desert. For a while, there is only the snow, my own breath, and the fish writhing at my feet. It is a strong fish, and it freezes slowly, dies hard, conscious of what pain and loss I cannot know. But for this moment I am moved, thinking how quickly I would succumb if our roles were reversed, and I breathed its water the way it now mouths the dark for oxygen. And I see before me the ice-crack, the Hornet plunging down. I float in the blue-blackness beneath the ice, my lungs hoarding a last breath, my heart beating its sad, panicked timpani.

At last the fish stops twitching, lies still, hardens into an S-shape. I kick it into the darkness, following the prescribed ritual. The stars spin overhead; the moon is the tip of a fillet knife low in the sky. Perhaps tomorrow, as is their custom, some Chippewa women will drag sleds across the lake and collect these fish that white men find too misshapen to eat. They will stack them up like cords of firewood, take them home, make them live, holy in the bellies of their children. Perhaps, just perhaps, that is enough, I think, and turn to the warmth of the shanty.

Back inside, the fishing is best described as American Standard: a fathead on a sinker-bobber rig jigged off the bottom. No fumbling after the right fly on a darkening stream as the mosquitoes rise in waves about your face and bats skim the twilight; no reading the shore and imagining bottom structure, sorting through a mass of treble hooks, obstinate as wasps, to find the right jig or spoon to coax a bass from its watery lair; no sleek, expensive sonar and radar and crackling radio and video cassettes of proper fishing techniques and down-riggers dragged at the computed depths.

Simply put the minnow on the hook, slipping the barb below the dorsal fin, skim the shell of ice, and watch the minnow and lead weight slowly sink into the viewer scope of the hole. Adjust the bobber. Lift the jiggle stick now and then, more when you first start and really believe that you will catch walleye this time. Then wait. And talk.

Pop psychologists and shrinks have made much ado in the last decade about how men don't communicate with each other, but perhaps it is that men just have unusual ways of communicating, as Tom and I do. For mostly we talk around subjects, circling as fish must suspicious baits. There are words, silences, glances, gestures, questions, sentences left dangling. Tom can say more with a shrug than anyone I know. So we talk of a marriage gone, the deaths of those we loved and whose dying we thought we could not bear. We talk of children, of yesterday, of tomorrow. We tell old jokes, recalling our own foolishness, the stories that over the years have grown around us, and in their retelling, fact and fiction have become indistinguishable. And we cannot contain the belly-aching laughter.

Later we stand outside in the snow. The sky is wild with stars, a riot of blazing light, as if a hand had dabbed, poured, then spread liquid fire across the void. The cold air sears our lungs as we gaze northward where pink shafts of light dance, wands of color shooting skyward off the polar ice. The frozen desert stretches away to a pine rim where a few cabin lights burn. We may catch no walleye, but we are relearning awe and wonder, that which is so often missing in our routine lives upon the planet.

We check our watches; it is past midnight. We should go. Warm beds await us. But we are hypnotized by the holes in which our bobbers float sheathed in ice. Stare long enough and the bobber seems to sink slowly in the hole. Blink and clear your head, and the bobber is still on the surface. Just a few more minutes, we think, just one more fresh minnow on the hook. The one o'clock run will start any minute now. The one-thirty run, any minute now. The two o'clock run ...

Suddenly, both our bobbers are down and we are shouting, pulling our lines up in handfuls of snarls. My fish makes a strong run. I think it must be an eight-pounder. Surely a wall-eye the way it fights. In the corner I hear Tom start to laugh. I turn as he hoists my bobber and line through his hole, hauling up behind it another writhing eelpout, both our hooks deep in its gullet.

There is nothing to do but laugh and pack and make our way home in the darkness, creeping the Hornet slowly across the wooden planks, eyes straining to make out the road markers as the wind blows clouds of snow across the lake. We are tired, yes, and fishless, true. But we have the memories of laughter, of the stories. Falling asleep, I see those cold stars blazing in the darkness and the blue hole in the ice, and find a peace there I can find nowhere else. I sleep as soundly as I have ever slept in my life.

STUART OSTHOFF

Stuart Osthoff is publisher of The Boundary Waters Journal, *a wilderness recreation, nature and conservation magazine covering The Boundary Waters Canoe Area Wilderness and Quetico Provincial Park. He and his wife, Michele, have restored a 100-year-old Finnish log home on 280 acres south of Ely, Minn. From there, they publish the magazine, raise their two boys, and operate one of the top sled dog sprint racing kennels in North America. Rather than equating success with discretionary income, Stuart defines success in terms of discretionary time. "At least that's how we justify enjoying more hunting, fishing, canoeing, camping and sled dogging than anyone has a right to."*

Reprinted by permission of the author and *The Boundary Waters Journal*.

Hunting with the Wolves

STUART OSTHOFF

" One thought continues to flood my mind: I can't believe what I just saw. Nobody else is going to believe it, either. "

I'm in a melancholy mood as I close out the final afternoon of Minnesota's deer season. It's been another great one, but I'm always sad to see it end. I know the chances of getting a mountable buck in my crosshairs at the eleventh hour are slim to none, but when you love this game as much as I do, it's easy to believe anything is possible. Even these final moments are significant in seeing me through the next three hundred fifty days. Overlooking a deep gorge connecting Blueberry Lake with a big bog, I finish my lunch, buckle on my fanny pack, and shoulder my rifle. Crossing the creek bottom and climbing the opposite ridge, I break out into a picturesque meadow.

"Four more hours and these bucks are safe for another year," I tell myself. Perhaps a hundred yards of birch and hazel brush separate the meadow from a ten-acre beaver pond. Suddenly, the somber, gray afternoon is shaken by a blood-curdling bawl, loud crashing of ice and splashing of water. In sixteen years of deer hunting this territory, I have never seen a timber wolf. Yet somehow I immediately know only one thing could create such a terror-filled moan. A deer is being attacked by wolves.

For the next four or five minutes, I hold my position, hoping the wolves will run what surely sounds like a Boone and Crockett buck right into my gun. But the struggle rages on out in the black, icy water of the beaver pond, and I decide to take a ringside seat. Darting and twisting through the brush, I reach a small, grassy knoll, undetected. Heart racing, finger on the safety of my Browning semi-automatic .308, I race up the knoll. Just before I crest the knoll, two brown-and-white wolves come bounding up the bank toward me. The first crosses ten yards in front of me, never sensing my presence. The second has a better angle. Our eyes meet; he whirls on a dime and sprints back out onto the ice.

My cover blown, I top out, wanting to get a shot at this "big buck" before he clears the water and reaches the woods. Four more wolves are on the ice watching the retreating wolf, searching for the source of his fright. They all see me and desert the mud-and-stick beaver dams for the shortest route to the far bank. Soon all five plunge through the ice into the frigid swamp water, frantically swimming and clawing for a foothold. But the ice just keeps breaking, and they bust their way through separate channels to the far shore. I'm sure they feel helpless and vulnerable, having gone from hunters to hunted so quickly.

Loud bawling from my side of the pond turns my attention back to the deer. About fifty yards ahead, I see the tall marsh grass whipping to and fro and hear another bawl, so I sprint toward that spot. At ten yards, I stop and flick off the safety. There is now no way the deer can reach the woods without giving me a shot. I creep forward, leading each step with my left foot, something I learned moving in on pointing bird dogs. It maintains balance for a right-handed shooter, eliminating the need to waste a half-second to shuffle the feet when the flush comes. In hunting, these split seconds make all the difference.

At ten feet, I peer over the grass, searching for antlers, especially big antlers. Like a giant jack-in-the-box, a big brown-and-white wolf springs up in front of me and dashes into the safety of the nearby woods. I'm not sure who is most surprised: the wolf, the deer, or me. For a few seconds I contemplate whether I would have been able to react with a killing shot at such close quarters had the wolf come at me. A person can't get any closer to a wolf before driving it from its freshly fallen prey. Fortunately, the wolf's instinctive fear of humans prevailed.

Still, I shudder while moving forward to look at the deer. It's a big doe, so I snap the safety back on, wondering if a bullet would bring her less pain. She is hyperventilating, struggling to catch her breath. She actually seems relieved to see this orange-clad, rifle-toting human standing over her. I see no hamstrung hocks, broken legs or exposed entrails. After I watch her for a minute, the doe gets her wind back, wobbles down to the beaver pond, and swims out into the middle through the broken-ice channel she had opened earlier. Half-submerged, she finds footing in the muck and surveys the scene. Only a very small amount of blood smears the grass where she had lain. I climb back onto the open knoll to watch her.

Soon, two wolves come out of the brush on the far bank and sit down on their haunches, watching both the deer and me. They are a hundred yards from me and half that distance from the doe. I scope them all for nearly ten minutes. All is at a standstill. Eventually, the doe recovers her strength and begins stomping her foot in the mud to elicit some response. She is completely alert. Finally, the wolves melt into the brush, and I retreat toward the meadow, letting the doe plainly see my exit, in hopes she will swim to my side, rather than leave the pond where the pack surely waits.

I swing south, still-hunting around the big bog, but the excitement of seeing the wolf pack in action makes it hard to concentrate. So I sit down to watch a few deer trails and contemplate the whole wild episode. One thought continues to flood my mind: I can't believe what I just saw. Nobody else is going to believe it, either. It still seems like just a dream.

I've heard wolves howling dozens of times in a decade and a half of deer hunting our place ten miles south of Ely. Usually, just before daybreak, the pack reassembles after having separated during the nightly hunt. A couple of times I have even heard wolves munching on a deer gut pile I've left the day before. Yet, somehow, they always come and go like gray ghosts, never letting me see them. Always there are tracks.

In twenty-five years of hunting whitetails, I've developed tremendous respect for their senses of smell, sight and hearing, all far superior to mine. But timber wolves are much more wary than deer. It's almost as if they have a sixth sense for detecting human intruders. It is tempting to believe it's only a matter of time before a hunter happens upon a pack with a deer. Yet, in talking to hunters, trappers and woodsmen who have spent their entire lives in wolf country, most have never seen what I just saw. I know I may never again experience a more inspiring predator-prey confrontation — a sobering thought for someone who lives to hunt, fish, paddle and hike.

After a couple of hours of chilly stump-sitting, I turn to more complicated thoughts. I suddenly realize the wolves and I were directly competing for that deer. Wolves kill for sustenance, a fundamental law of nature easy for people to understand. I hunt deer for sport, something only other hunters really understand.

While I suspected the deer might be a big buck, I wanted it as badly as the wolves did. If it had carried a trophy rack, I surely would have shot it. I wonder what I would have done had I known sooner that it was a doe. Would I have intervened to save the deer or just let nature run its course?

My leaving this deer to the wolves represents a major advance in deer hunter attitudes. Just a generation ago, it would have been incumbent upon me to pound four or five of those wolves into that beaver pond, and I know I easily could have. Years ago, it was perceived as a simple equation: fewer wolves, more deer, better hunting. A wolf in the Superior National Forest kills fifteen to twenty deer per year. Therefore, the logic goes, I could have saved up to one hundred deer by killing the wolves. Projecting that out over my little corner of the whitetail world, my area might then hold ten antlered bucks rather than seven or eight.

But neither predator nor prey has an easy life in this forest. Animal populations cycle up and down depending on many factors: weather, habitat, disease and others. Because the human mind focuses on the welfare of individuals, many people mistakenly apply this to the animal world. It is difficult for many of us to accept that in the overall scheme, individual deer, or deer hunters, don't count for much of anything.

The sun has set on the deer season, and pockets of brush are now lost in dark shadows. I'm forced to concede there will be no more excitement this year. There have been many highlights. My love for this game just grows deeper every year.

This is the first deer season since my father passed away. By the time I was twelve, Dad had drilled gun safety and sportsmanship into my soul. The lessons of self-discipline and responsibility he taught me while hunting were a stronger influence than eight years of college and a dozen employment stops. I never violated his trust, and I know he's smiling down on me today for understanding that the timber wolf is what makes deer hunting in the Boundary Waters so very special.

When not practicing law, Ted Nelson Lundrigan wanders the hills of his rural county, "drawing deeply upon the hospitality of those

TED NELSON LUNDRIGAN

who live there and adding to the idle curiosity of those who don't." He has fought a war, helped raise four children, buried one of them, divorced once, married twice, trained four dogs and, while waiting for grouse season to open, tries to find some excuse to shoot one of his shotguns whenever possible. His stories, written under the pen name Ted Nelson, have appeared in Shooting Sportsman, Pointing Dog Journal, Gun Dog, Wildfowl, *and* Sporting Classics. *His first book,* Hunting the Sun: A Passion for Grouse, *was published in spring 1997 by Countrysport Press.*

Tin Fins and Lead Bellies

TED NELSON LUNDRIGAN

> **Most time spent fishing is not fishing at all, just waiting. If the spear hole has a bright, sandy bottom and a few weeds, the background provides some diversion. A few perch swim in and out, stopping on occasion to nose the decoy that swims around in little circles, lifted by a string attached to a small stick.**

A lake frozen from corner to corner has nowhere to go when the weather is making ice. Some thing has to give, and it does. The ice cracks and grinds, groaning from the effort of it. It is a big eardrum to a dark house fisherman out on the surface. It magnifies every sound.

Sometimes the big cracks run for miles. When they do, the sound is not like a crack at all. It is a long, drawn out vibration, as if all the strings of a giant harp were struck at once. In the warm darkness of a fish house, all imaginings are possible, especially to the twelve-year-old that I was in those days. The green, flickering light of the water in the spearing hole was a campfire, and the mutterings and moans of the ice were lions circling the thorn ring.

I suppose it was the presence of the spear that incubated these African imaginings, or, maybe, too many *Jungle Jim* comic books. Regardless, in the moist, warm darkness of a fish house, all things were possible. After all, there were alligators swimming in the waters, big green ones called northern pike that slashed in from the side and seized the little red-and-white decoy. I can't speak from experience because even this many years later I have never had it happen, but I believe a lion jumping into the campfire light couldn't startle a sleepy boy much worse.

This was my father's winter activity, and that of his friends and fellow sportsmen. When I was a boy, the culture of fish houses, spearing fish and carving wooden decoys was second only to the nine days of deer hunting. They kept their little shanties in a pasture not far from the lake. They were about four by six feet on the floor and about six-and-a-half feet tall, just the right size for the back of a pickup. The spear hole was an open rectangle in one corner, stretching almost to the other side, leaving a ledge for ice skimmer buckets or a small boy on a stool. Behind the hole and next to the wall was a small, black metal box with a door in front and a stovepipe rising through the roof. Wires ran from each side of the pipe, securing it from an accidental bump. The stove was nailed to the floor so that when the house was tipped on its skis to be towed to the fishing site the whole works wouldn't come apart and fly around inside. The wire was also the clothesline for wet mittens, jackets, caps, and gloves.

The first order of business in late fall after the deer hunt was to clear the house of summer renters. We swept out mouse nests and plugged new holes in the old Masonite or particle board walls with tar and small tin patches. The inside of the fish house had to be as pitch black as we could make it. Light might sneak around a stovepipe or twinkle through a hole and spook a wary northern pike as it lurked outside the spearing hole and examined the little tin-finned fish.

Then we took the cigar box of small wooden fish out of the big blue pail. All along the top rail of the wall, right above the spearing hole, was a row of long wire hooks. Every old decoy had its place. Like soldiers after the charge, each took its spot in the line: The peeled green one that brought in the big pike two years ago, the little yellow fat fish that couldn't swim right. Each was hung and each story retold.

These veterans were joined by bright replacements. My brother, my dad and I carved two or three new ones every year, tin fins and lead bellies, each one painted to a certain blend of traditional colors. Red and white to attract the whitefish. Yellow and red for the northern pike. Green for a change. The shape of the body was unique to each carver. Some liked them long and slim, others short and stubby. The top and side fins were cut from tin cans with a tab to be inserted through a slot cut into the side of the wooden body. A side fin might be long like a short wing, or it might be stubby, in which case there were usually two fins on each side.

The tail and top fin added that certain attitude necessary in all top contenders.

A skilled carver made his top fin out of bent wire. Along the leading edge he made small sharp curves so that the swivel would clip in one place or another and allow it to float level and straight. Others made a big flat blade and drilled or punched holes for the clip. The trick was to remember which hole on each little fish gave it the right angle.

The tail was for artistic license. Some favored the two-tip fish tail, some the caudal (or tadpole) style. A true whittler carved the tail as part of the body and hoped he had not given it too much rudder, or worse, not enough. A decoy had to stay within the four corners of the spearing hole to do its job.

My dad favored cutting a small rectangle into the belly of the bait. The tab from each of the tin fins could be pushed through the outside into the opening and then hot lead poured in to seal the hole. Some carvers drilled openings for the weight, but Dad sort of sniffed at that as a shortcut. Tin fins, lead bellies and brass tack eyes. No shortcuts for serious business.

A sack of small cut wood was thrown into the house along with the backless spearing chair and a couple of folding stools. An axe to cut the ice hole and a chisel to finish the job and shape the hole were followed by the spear.

We never threw a spear down or banged it around. All the ones I ever saw were handmade, each with a wooden scabbard. The tines were long and graceful, sharp as razors with barbs on the inside edges. Sometimes the handle was a solid piece of iron rod, but more often, it was hollow, weighted at the spear end and tipped with a wooden handle. About six to

eight feet of cord came out of the end of the handle to be teth-
ered to the chair leg.

"Why don't you tie it to your leg, Dad?" I once asked.

He drew strongly on his unfiltered Camel, the glow from
its tip adding orange light to the dark house. He blew the
smoke toward the spear and laughed quietly. "A few years
ago, several actually, I was fishing over on the Whitefish
banks. The ice was booming and moaning as it was a very
cold day. I had set up my house among a group of others. As
it turned out, one of these houses was a rental from a nearby
resort. I heard a big crack coming across the lake sizzling and
thrumming. It passed close by my house, and the water rose
and fell as the ice moved. Someone started screaming, and I
heard a door kicked open. Then I heard a few quick steps and
some more screaming. 'Help! Help! It's going down!' the
voice yelled. I opened my door and saw this guy lying on the
ice clawing and crying, trying to pull himself and his fish
house, I guess, to the shore. I got up and walked over. He was
being held in place by the spear cord, which was tied to his
foot. The spear, in turn, was crossways in the open door. I
walked over to his fish house and pulled the spear loose. He
got to his feet and ran all the way to the shore with the spear
bouncing and dragging behind."

"Why was he so scared?" I asked.

Dad laughed again and coughed for a minute. "I looked
inside. That big crack came right through his hole. He
thought he was going down."

Dad was a natural story teller, and now, warmed up with
my laughter, he told about another fisherman who was scared
out of his wits. I suspect the story was an old one, but I have
owned two fine black Labrador retrievers, and if it didn't
happen, it could have.

"Jack was a big, happy black Lab," Dad recalled. "He
made himself a regular pest around our little village of fish
houses and wasn't averse to taking a fish from outside our
houses and carrying it to his master. On this day, however, he
was inside watching the hole, as dogs sometimes do. A fish
came in, and his owner threw the spear at it. He made the hit

and brought the fish back up to the top, where in its flopping back and forth it fell free from the tines and into the hole.

"Jack went after it. In a flash he was gone under the water and out of sight. His master went nuts. 'Jack! Jack!' he yelled. As he ran outside, he was met by the guy from the house next door, who was screaming just as loud in terror. Jack had come up in the guy's hole, blowing, black, and spraying water! Now, Jack was very happy to see his master, and likewise I'm sure. But the poor soul from next door had been having a slow day until that point and damned near had a coronary."

Ice cracks and black Labs weren't the only things that surfaced in spearing holes. Muskrats are industrious little furbearers even in the dead of winter. Given the urge and a long, clean expanse of underwater ice, a rat will swim against the underside, pushing a big air bubble ahead of him as a scuba tank.

By the time my brother got his driver's license, I had taken possession of the old fish house and we had a second one. He and I were traveling about the country, moving our houses to new and different water. Following a tip, we placed both our houses on a small, dark-bottomed bog lake. It was a crushing bore. The water was dark, the bottom muddy, and the pike absent.

Most time spent fishing is not fishing at all, just waiting. If the spear hole has a bright, sandy bottom and a few weeds, the background provides some diversion. A few perch swim in and out, stopping on occasion to nose the decoy that swims around in little circles, lifted by a string attached to a small stick. The stick, in turn, is tied to a tether so that it can be held at a certain depth and dropped when a fish swims in to grab the bait. A few more flicks on the decoy stick had not produced any more fish than in the previous two hours. Only the moan of the wind around the corners of the house and the slow ticking of the stove provided company. The bottom was black, the little wooden fish suspended against a dark-green curtain. But I had nothing more important to do and was content with that and some self-serving adolescent thoughts about girls and fast cars.

Then the water in my spearing hole burst with a *whoosh* and startled me backwards. A wet and slippery muskrat splashed onto the floor between my feet. Size is a relative thing. At fifty feet a muskrat is small, especially with all outdoors surrounding it. At five feet it is not too big, but rather, too close. At five inches it is both too big and too close. I recoiled against the wall and stabbed at the rat with my spear. It feinted and bit the spear, and with a hiss retreated farther into the house. I stabbed again, and it dodged. I was between the rat and the water; it was between me and the door. It retreated still farther, rising on its hind legs. Suddenly, there was a puff of steam and the odor of burnt fur. It had backed up against the stove.

The rat was between my feet and into the water quicker than I could blink. I groped for the chair and sat down, my knees shaking, sweating with exertion and fear. I opened the door and, braced by the cold winter air, walked over to my brother's fish house. He looked at my face and said: "What happened to you?" I sat down on his extra stool and related the story. After a bit, he stopped laughing and replied, "Good thing they don't eat meat."

The best part of the season lasts about as long as Christmas vacation. After that, the January cold fills the spear hole with so much ice that it is hard to break through with the long-handled chisel. The house has to be moved off the site and the hole recut with an axe. The house is then reset over the opening, the sides banked with snow, and the stove fire lit. The fish stop running and are few and far between. For a couple of weekends the spear fishermen try to find new spots, but the effort of pulling the house, cutting the hole and resetting everything gets to be too much.

The worst year I ever saw was the first year Dad rented a chain saw to cut the hole. He was sure that would be the answer to the hard work of late season ice. It was an old yellow McCulloch, as hard to start as a wheezy Buick with a straight-eight motor, but he got it going and with a broad grin cut into the lake with the full length of the blade. He cut all four sides and never struck water.

Dad, my brother and I stared in astonishment. We broke the cube out of its mold. He struck the bottom of the hole a few times with our chisel.

"Still solid," he said grimly. Then, with valor born of desperation, he started the saw again and stepped into the hole. He cut down a second time, full length, first one side, then the next, until he had gone around. Still no water. The cutting bar was twenty inches long. Still undeterred by forty inches of ice, he tried a third time in just one corner. It came out dry. "Boys," he said as he shut off the sputtering saw, "four feet of ice is my limit."

Some years the lake would freeze with hard, black ice, pure and dark. You could look through it to the bottom. The cracks were marbled walls and on top there would be small piles of snow here and there like small spots of frosting. We had an old Willys Jeep that on a good day could attain the heady speed of forty-five miles per hour. My brother had his driver's license, and he would floor it until it was wound as tight as it could go. Then he would spin the steering wheel, and we would go round and round in the finest carnival ride on earth. After a few turns, he would let me take the wheel, and by the time I was old enough to take my driver's license exam, I had enough experience at steering out of and into skids to teach the course.

The trick was to stay away from ice heaves. When lake ice buckles, one side goes up and the other slides down. It makes a great ramp for high-speed jumps, if you know which side to come from. If you don't, the rear tires and axle stay with the heave and the rest of the car continues on. I learned early in my ice driving that turning the wheel often accomplishes nothing. It was the classic application of the law of physics that says an object in motion tends to stay in motion.

The other side of that law says that objects at rest stay at rest. My high school pal, Bucky, was very good at physics. His father was not. Bucky loved to ice fish, and so did his good friend, Jimmy. They each had a fish house and often placed them close together so they could socialize and compare notes. Bucky's dad was a great one for ice driving. He knew, as did we all, that a car coming across the ice made lots of noise when heard from inside a fish house. The water magnified the sound, and a passing car sounded a lot closer than it really was. He decided one afternoon to put a little excitement into Bucky's fishing.

I have wondered from time to time when exactly he turned the wheel. It was probably a quarter-mile from Bucky's house, but the ice was dark and smooth, and his little French car was zipping right along. It had front-wheel drive, rare in those days, and he was proud of its road ability. He steered one way, then the other, but onward charged the pride of Paris. A cruise missile could not have been more committed.

At some point he knew it was useless and leaned on the horn (at this point in the story, Bucky would always break up in laughter). Jimmy opened the door of his house, and he and Bucky looked on in stunned amazement. The French car zoomed past, horn blaring, driver screaming, to hit the hapless fish house dead center. Pieces scattered into the air, and the stove exploded into a wonderful burst of smoke and ash. The car continued on, spinning around until it came to rest, with the roof of Bucky's shanty lying on top. His dad sat stunned and frozen at the wheel.

The two boys put on their coats and walked in little short penguin-style steps across the slick surface. Bucky rapped at the car window. His dad looked at him.

"What are doing?" Bucky asked. His dad put the car in gear and very slowly drove off the ice.

A spearing hole was my window into the freshwater world for all my teen years. Through it I saw walleyes swim slow and green along the bottom, their white-tipped fins the only thing distinguishing them from the common sucker. How many times did I plot how to hit one with the wooden end of the spear in such a way as I could stun it? On a bright day, the whitefish might run in schools, and three or even four could come smooth and fast into the hole. But for sheer excitement, nothing could beat a big northern pike.

First, the small fish would scatter away, leaving the decoy on its tether, utterly still. My heart would start to pound. I slid the spear into the water, but kept its five tines up against the ice so the fish could not see it. The pike would be circling the decoy, out of sight, beyond the border of the hole. It was hard to know just what to do. Maybe one more twitch of the decoy would trigger a charge, and maybe it would scare the fish away. If I got down low and peered out under the ice, I might just get a glimpse of a smooth green shadow or the flick of a red tail.

Then, he was there, nose pressed against the decoy. Or perhaps he seized it and swam out again. It would only be a second, or maybe two, and he would drop away to the left or right, never to return. The spear went deeper, and because of the light-bending quality of the water, appeared to kink in the direction of the fish. I tried to hit the fish right behind the head. Otherwise, it would struggle and fight the spear. A five-pound fish looked big, a ten-pounder looked like a whale, and anything bigger looked like a bad dream.

The stroke was never a throw. It was like a pool cue shot, smooth and straight in a long push. Sometimes the hit took place right in front of me, and I just hauled the fish up and into the house. Other times, the spear was out and gone under the ice, and I didn't know if I had a fish until I got hold of the handle. Either way, the return had to be quick because once I had a grip on the spear, the fish had leverage and could rip itself loose.

Up he would come, out of the water, then onto the floor, where I drove the spear down into the wood. Now the fish was mine. I would walk around the thrashing tail, kick open the door and lift the fish out into the frigid air. A few sharp shakes on the spear and it was flopping on the ice. Tradition now dictated I slam the door shut. No reason to be quiet. No sir, I had a fish, and the others around me had to know it!

It has been thirty years. If any part of our old fish houses is still in that pasture, it might be the steel ski runners, or maybe the rusty corner of a stove. Dad hurt his back about the time my brother and I finished college. Then the war came on the heels of my graduation, and I never got back with a broom and a bag of nails and some tar. I still have the old blue pail, and most of the decoys. The spear is in my mother's garage rafters, along with the ice chisel, each blade in its own wooden scabbard.

I think about starting up again, but I would have to do it alone. The culture is gone. Dad died a few years ago, and my brother is far away. And being alone with my thoughts in a warm, dark place that booms and cracks is not as appealing as it once was. Sometimes I remember that guy clawing and scratching on the ice, and it is not so funny any more.

Jim Klobuchar is a long-time writer-adventurer known to Midwest newspaper readers through his daily column in the Minneapolis Star Tribune. *He is the author of fifteen books, several of which chronicle his world of action as a mountaineer, bicyclist, cross-country skier, and leader of hiking expeditions from the Himalayas to Africa. Now retired from daily journalism, he is still active as an author of books and explorer of the high and remote country. In 1984 he received the National Society of Newspaper Columnists' award as the country's outstanding columnist for newspapers over 100,000 circulation. In 1986 he was named a finalist in NASA's journalist in space project before it was put on hold in the aftermath of the space shuttle Challenger accident. He lives in Minnetonka, Minn.*

JIM KLOBUCHAR

Reprinted by permission of the author and the *Minneapolis Star Tribune*. This selection appears in the book, *Wild Places and Gentle Breezes*.

A Chorale of Wolves at Midnight

JIM KLOBUCHAR

Another wolf howl, this one filling the tent with its unearthly siren, from a distance of no more than a hundred yards. Jesus. They were in my front yard, just off the shoreline from where I was camped in a grove of cedars.

The concert began ten minutes before midnight. Its virtuoso soloist was the leader of the pack, piercing the motionless air with a howl that drifted from the ice of East Bearskin Lake into the crowns of the high Norway pines miles away. There is no sound that so starkly defines the winter wilderness as a wolf baying in the night. For any human intruder within earshot, it stifles the breath and grabs the skin. It evokes a tormented loneliness and a sense of menace too vivid to be appeased by the calmer wisdom of the woods.

A man lodging alone in a tent beside the frozen lake may understand the lore and find it reassuring, although not wholly convincing. They must have been a quarter-mile away or so when the head vocalist and the rest of his chorale began. At that distance, I did not find the performance disagreeable. Only the leader howled during this movement; the others barked and yapped. It must be a sight. Imagine. A wolf pack in congregation under an almost-full moon and flaming starlight on a February night in the Boundary Waters Canoe Area.

I struggled out of my double sleeping bag, unzipped the front panel of the tent, and looked out on the ice to the east. They were in shadow in a bay, but their forms were visible, five or six, moving here and there. There was another howl, more yapping and snuffling. The temperature must have been fifteen to twenty below zero, heading for twenty-five below. No thermometer was necessary. The suddenness of the pain in the fingertips, touching cold nylon and metal, was an accurate substitute for mercury. So was the instantly stiff hair in the nostrils and the stunning light show of the northern sky pouring down on the soft white velvet of the lake's snow cover.

The wolves stopped. Nothing moved or sounded over the great sweep of the imprisoned lake and the forests beyond. Goodbye, wolves. For a moment there, I suspected the erudition of the scientific wolf watchers, who believe that the nocturnal wailing isn't wailing at all, but rather a declaration of joy by the pack. A family sing-along. Not a hostile note in it, the wise ones insist.

I apologized to the scientists for being momentarily deceived. So doing, I zipped back in and dozed for fifteen minutes. Roll over now because a rib of snow under the tent floor has formed an uncompromising neck-to-kneebone ridge of ice that can't be ignored and has to be outwitted. Doze a few minutes more.

Another wolf howl, this one filling the tent with its unearthly siren, from a distance of no more than a hundred yards.

Jesus.

They were in my front yard, just off the shoreline from where I was camped in a grove of cedars. The barking seemed more urgent. That might have been the power of suggestion, but there was nothing imaginary about the decibel count. It was running off the scale.

Wolves' admirers maintain there has never been a documented case of a wolf attacking a human in northern Minnesota. As one of the admirers, I've never challenged the premise. At this moment, however, I thought the record just might be incomplete. Maybe a few undocumented cases? I tugged out of my downy cocoon again and trained a flashlight on my available armory: a Swiss army knife and four

aluminum mini-pots from my cooking set. If it came to battle, I was going to defend myself by rattling aluminum pots.
The prospect, if they were aware of it, did not appear to ter-
rify my visitors outside. The yelping accelerated. Were they
simply inquisitive? Were they sociable? How long had they
gone without a square meal?

I don't think I'll ever know. Trying to unzip the front door
of the tent again, I set off a racket that must have scattered
the wolves either in fright or bafflement, because when I
looked out on the lake again, it was flooded with innocent
moonlight and nothing more. Something cracked in the
woods behind me. It captured my undivided attention, but it
was no creature, that. The subzero air was the performer this
time, playing its percussions with the saps and knots. I was
left to the night and its soundless musings. I slept, occasionally.

I would have slept more in the Boundary Waters in summer, when it is the settled habitat of the recreational canoeist
and the loon-seeker. Traveling alone in winter takes a different kind of orientation of the mind and an adjustment for the
flesh. By most of the values of touring and wayfaring, it is an
unnatural act. It might impose some risk, and it certainly will
present some discomfort.

One part of the wilderness experience is its pageant of
exotic sights and sounds, its remoteness and purities, and
therefore its grace and beauty. The other is the chemistry it
creates within the traveler. The experience can be vast geo-
graphically and powerful, but it is not truly wild nature
unless it bestows on the traveler one of its deepest gifts,
which is the intimacy and the kinship one feels in its presence.

On a winter's day, or night, it may be harsh or lovely, con-
vivial or wrenching. But it is wild. And this adds another
dimension. In the twentieth century, we live in unbroken
interdependence. Every day, we see hundreds or thousands of
people, hear hundreds or thousands of voices. But what if,
every three or four years or so — and say you had the incli-
nation, equipment, time, and possibly the required fleeting

spark of irrationality — you could spend twenty-four or forty-eight hours without seeing another person, hearing another voice?

Would it be worth the quizzical eyebrows of your friends?

Why, yes, assuming you were discreet enough to avoid the open water and to resist the impulse to schuss down a portage slope. The risk in skiing and snowshoeing the frozen lakes and their portages for three days is marginal if the traveler is equipped and reasonably seasoned.

The time I skied onto Bearskin's lanky east-west lake, a trailing wind energetically shoved me over the hard pack. It was almost like sailing. I dug a pole into the scrabble and glided with a stroke, leaving me awkwardly unbalanced until I quickly leaned on the other ski. Once a quartering breeze did catch my backpack and almost flipped me. The world's stubbiest spinnaker.

Poles and skis usually make creaking, squalling sounds slicing through the snow. The snow cover of East Bearskin was so hard it produced grinding, hollow noises of rapidly rising timbres as my body pressures shifted, like water filling up an empty jar. If you ski cross-country, those sensations stick, because they are your companions for hours.

The thin crescent of Alder Lake's eastern arm broadened into the main basin, familiar to hundreds of summer canoers and campers. For a day or two in winter, it belonged to just one. It is a heady idea, if not totally accurate. As visitors we come not as proprietors but as witnesses. And while we may experience a quiet exultation being alone in the forest and coursing the lakes, we can never be totally at ease in this place in winter.

If it storms, we should be ready. There is a time for gawking and investigation, but when traveling alone in winter, one moves under constant imperatives that approach the force of religious codes. Do not squander body warmth, and stay dry.

So I would put my camp in midday on the site of a summer campground beside the portage between Alder and Canoe lakes. I raised my two-man Timberline tent twenty-five or thirty yards away, rested inside for half an hour, aired the sleeping bags in the crotches of a couple of pine trees, and then skied uncluttered for two hours into little Pierz Lake to the east.

Some old moose tracks plodded through a bay there, and a weasel's precise little prints laced a small section near shore on the other side of the lake. Otherwise, it was barren of clues to wildlife. The probable truth was that there wasn't much around. You can call the winter animal life in the Boundary Waters wild, but you can't call it stupid. Much of what there is stays close to civilization, the few resorts open the year round, private homes whose owners make occasional visits in the winter.

Should the traveler be disappointed? Hardly. The wolves can fill the void adequately at midnight. A solitary glimpse into the Northwoods, even only three days of it, tantalizes the intruder with games and mind pictures. I snowshoed on some of my explorations, plodding deep into the woods where no other human was likely to have come this winter. I had a rough destination, but mostly it was a pleasure cruise. Wind whooshed through the pines with those shifting surges and moods that give it an invisible personality. The temptation to imagine some kind of message in its sounds is irresistible. A welcome, a warning, a private hymn the traveler might detect but could not possibly interpret. That may be why the wind in the pines is so captivating. It seems to put the visitor on the verge of understanding, and it mingles its own yearnings with the human's. But it also beguiles and evades. Then it is silent, and the enigma remains.

Without company, snowshoers conjure those fantasies, creating companions out of the trees in a way that gently mocks our search for solitude. If we lack the biologist's precise eye to identify all of the life and phenomena around us, we will often start looking at the woods allegorically. Sooner or later we all assign human values to the part of nature that is important to us. We do that out of fear, enjoyment or reverence. The sun is healing or the thunderclouds are malevolent. The wind is saucy. It is a harmless mental exercise that reminds us how desperately at times we want to immerse ourselves in the magic of wild nature.

So if there is nothing wrong with fantasy in the forest, what was it doing today? It was full of pranks and teasings. An overhanging branch of a big black spruce forced me to scrunch as I passed underneath. I made the move flawlessly, without touching a twig. I straightened up in self-congratulatory attitude, and as I did, an unseen second branch lifted my cap cleanly. Was that some kind of reprimand? Did I make a social blunder coming into this woodsy cathedral with my head covered?

Two yards farther on, a bough swatted me in the run. And so it went. I skied back into camp a few minutes after five o'clock, spread the sleeping bags on a foam mat and aluminum-sheeted space blanket, and lit the small cooking stove. Now the chores. First to the creek, where the water rippled and chattered between great snow-duned logs. To reach it, I slid into the snowshoes and spraddled around until I was able to balance on two logs and dip my cooking pots into the water. Don't fall here, baby. They might bring you back with a Zamboni from the ice center.

It was a fairly deft operation at that. Pleased, I maneuvered the big Alaskan snowshoes through the fallen timber and boulders, bearing two water pots like an ungainly Gunga Din. Almost back onto the portage trail, I caught a hidden root with the tail of a snowshoe. Both pots flew into the snow. Back up the creek.

This time, I outflanked the root and arrived at my crude little kitchen with both pots brimming. In ten minutes, I had boiling water and prepared now to answer the day's most provocative question: Can freeze-dried sausage patties be made edible by swashing them for five minutes in boiling water in their plastic bags?

I emptied the water, as directed, and bit into the first of four sausage patties. To put it modestly, they were marvelous. At 5:45 p.m., I slid into my sleeping bag. The sun was dying beyond the pine crowns, and there was nothing to do but outlast the night. I zipped to my nose and listened. Every ten minutes or so, something would crack, a tree vein in the below-zero air, my knee joint from the cramping, the ice far out on the lake, maybe something else. At about the time I had it all figured, sleep crept up.

For fifteen minutes. Then another crack. The northland on a winter night is wild, and unforgettable, but not always poetic.

It is, however, almost always suspenseful.

Far Back

ORVAL LUND

in one
of the valleys
of the Whitewater
within
a winter woods
of skeletal
poplar and oak
that stand
knee-deep
in crusted
snow
deep
in a hole
of slow
flowage
beneath a
sky
of white
ice
lies
a brown trout,
its sides
dark
its orange spots
obscured
barely
moving
a tail flip
now
a fin flare
then
just
enough

to stay
stable
only by
concentrating
very
hard
can I
imagine
its gills
ever
so slowly
opening
and
closing
it feeds
little
in the cold
slow
water
its world is
gel
it lives on
fat
from summer
and on
something
else
deep
in winter
myself
I live on
dreams
of summer.

Previously published in *Minnesota Monthly*,
reprinted from *Take Paradise*, a chapbook from Dacotah Territory Press,
and forthcoming in *Casting Lines*, New Rivers Press, 1999.

ABOUT THE POETS

Poems for the section-opening pages and closing page of Minnesota Seasons *were written by* Orval Lund and Larry M. Gavin.

ORVAL LUND

Orval Lund grew up on the prairie in northwestern Minnesota, where he went after northern pike in the local river and rabbits in the popple woods. Eventually, he earned his master's degree at the University of Arizona and his master of fine arts from Vermont College. He has taught English at Winona State University since 1968 but is now spending a year teaching in Japan. Orval has published his poetry widely in literary magazines and two chapbooks, *Take Paradise* and *Ordinary Days*, both from Dacotah Territory Press. A recent winner of the Minnesota Voices Competition, his book, *Casting Lines*, will be published by New Rivers Press in 1999. An avid fly fisherman, grouse hunter, and deer hunter, Orval lives with his wife Michele in the bluffs around Winona. They have two grown sons.

LARRY M. GAVIN

Larry M. Gavin was born and raised in Austin, Minn., and lived for a time in Hinckley and Belview. His work has appeared in *Gray's Sporting Journal*, *Fly Rod and Reel*, *Gun Dog*, and many other publications. He won the 1995 Bread Loaf poetry prize for his poem "Ice Fishing at Winter Solstice." He is now a field editor specializing in poetry for *Midwest Fly Fishing* magazine. In summer, he is a fly-fishing instructor on the Missouri River in Montana; in autumn, he hunts waterfowl and upland game throughout Minnesota. He lives and teaches in Faribault. He and his wife, Patty, have a son, Fergus, and two springer spaniels, Ivy and Molly.

Also from
The Cabin Bookshelf

*These fine books are available
at your favorite bookstore.*

... of Woodsmoke
and Quiet Places

JERRY WILBER

Jerry Wilber presents a full year's worth of daily reflections on the outdoors and on life in the mythical North Country town of Lost Lake. Wilber's insights amuse and inspire, and along the way provide hints on how to be a better hunter, citizen, angler, camper, canoeist, cook, parent, spouse, friend.

400 pages   *hardcover*   *$25.95*
ISBN 0-9653381-1-8

Notes From
Little Lakes

MEL ELLIS

Mel Ellis describes how
he and his wife and their
five daughters (The Rebels)
turned a tract of pasture-
land into a haven for trees,
flowers, and wildlife. In
the lore of nature and the
environment, *Little Lakes*
is as familiar and as important as Aldo Leopold's
Sand County.

280 pages, hardcover
$23.95
ISBN 0-9653381-0-X

The Land,
Always the Land

MEL ELLIS

Never have the sights,
sounds, and moods of the
seasons been captured more
vividly than in this collection of writings by Mel
Ellis. Ellis leads us through
the year, month by month,
drawing us into a world we
often miss amid the swirl of
daily life. After reading this
book, you will see the
world anew on your trips
to the countryside and in
your daily travels across
town.

280 pages, hardcover
$23.95
ISBN 0-9653381-2-6